Gooseberry Patch Co.

Sweet & Simple

A Country Store In Your Mailbox ®

Gooseberry Patch
600 London Road
Department Book
Delaware, OH 43015
★
1·800·854·6673
gooseberrypatch.com

Copyright 2002, Gooseberry Patch 1-888052-96-1
First Printing, February, 2002

How To Subscribe

Would you like to receive
"A Country Store in Your Mailbox®"?
For a 2-year subscription to our 96-page
Gooseberry Patch catalog, simply send $3.00 to:

Gooseberry Patch ★ P.O. Box 190 ★ 600 London Road ★ Delaware, Ohio 43015

Contents

Dedication

For all our dearest
friends, you make
life sweet!

Appreciation

Thanks so much for sharing your favorite
recipes...you're the icing on the cake!

Peanut Butter Jumbos

*Julie Anthony
Homeworth, OH*

Everyone loves peanut butter and chocolate!

1/4 c. butter, softened
1 c. brown sugar, packed
1 c. sugar
1-1/2 c. creamy peanut butter
3 eggs
2 t. baking soda

1 t. vanilla extract
4-1/2 c. quick-cooking oats,
   uncooked
1 c. chocolate chips
1 c. candy-coated chocolate
   mini-baking bits

Cream butter, sugars, peanut butter and eggs in a large mixing bowl; blend in baking soda, vanilla and oats. Fold in chocolate chips and mini candy-coated bits; drop by tablespoonfuls onto greased baking sheets. Bake at 350 degrees for 15 to 20 minutes. Makes about 1-1/2 dozen.

*Broken cookies don't have calories.
-Unknown*

That's the Way the Cookie Crumbles

Butterscotch Cookies

Karen Harris
Delaware, OH

A sure winner...this recipe won a ribbon at our county fair.

1/2 c. butter, softened
3/4 c. sugar
3/4 c. brown sugar, packed
2 eggs
1 t. vanilla extract
1-1/2 c. all-purpose flour

1 t. salt
1 t. baking soda
12-oz. pkg. butterscotch chips
6-oz. pkg. toffee bits
1 c. chopped pecans

Cream butter with sugars; add eggs and vanilla. In another mixing bowl, sift together dry ingredients; blend into sugar mixture. Fold in chips, toffee pieces and pecans; chill dough at least 30 minutes. Roll dough into 1-1/2 inch balls; place on ungreased baking sheets at least 2 inches apart. Bake at 325 degrees for 9 to 12 minutes. Makes 5 to 6 dozen.

Fill a white paper lunch bag with bite-size cookies or mini muffins. Fold the top over and trim with decorative-edged scissors. Tucked inside the kids' school backpacks, they'll find a sweet treat they can share!

Oatmeal Crinkles

Krista Starnes
Beaufort, SC

*So delicious, my husband can't wait for them to cool...he eats them
as soon as they come out of the oven.*

1-1/4 c. sugar, divided
1 t. cinnamon
1 c. shortening
1 c. brown sugar, packed
2 eggs
1 t. vanilla extract
1 t. almond extract

2 c. all-purpose flour
1 t. baking powder
1 t. baking soda
1 t. salt
2-1/2 c. long-cooking oats,
  uncooked
1-1/2 c. raisins

Combine 1/4 cup sugar and cinnamon together; set aside. Cream
shortening, remaining sugar, brown sugar, eggs and extracts
together in a large mixing bowl; set aside. In another mixing bowl,
combine remaining ingredients; stir well. Add to sugar mixture; mix
well. Roll into walnut-size balls; roll in sugar and cinnamon mixture.
Place 2 inches apart on ungreased baking sheets; bake at
350 degrees for 10 minutes. Cool on baking sheet for 2 minutes;
remove to cool on wire rack. Makes about 5 dozen.

*A small ice cream scoop is so
handy when making drop
cookies...just scoop the dough
from the bowl and release
it onto the cookie
sheet. So easy!*

That's the Way the Cookie Crumbles

Ezra's Sugar Cookies

*Terry Ross
Converse, TX*

Use almond or lemon extract for a different taste.

1 c. butter, softened
1 c. sugar
1 t. vanilla extract

1 egg
2 t. baking powder
3 c. all-purpose flour

Cream butter and sugar together; blend in vanilla and egg. In another mixing bowl, combine baking powder and flour; add one cup at a time to sugar mixture, blending well. Roll out on a lightly floured surface to 1/8-inch thickness; cut into desired shapes. Bake on ungreased baking sheets at 400 degrees for 6 to 7 minutes; cool and frost, if desired. Makes about 2 dozen.

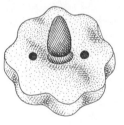

Creamy Frosting

*Becky Sykes
Gooseberry Patch*

Homestyle vanilla frosting...yummy on sugar cookies.

6 T. butter, softened
1-1/2 c. powdered sugar
2 T. whipping cream

3/4 t. vanilla extract
Optional: food coloring

Combine butter, powdered sugar, cream and vanilla together in a medium mixing bowl; blend on low speed of electric mixer until smooth. Divide frosting among 2 or 3 small bowls; tint to desired color. Use immediately. Makes one cup.

A balanced diet is a cookie in each hand.
-Unknown

Twist Cookies

Virginia Cook
Fairfield, CT

*The prettiest cookies...sprinkle with colored sugar
for extra sparkle.*

1 c. butter, softened
1-1/2 c. sugar
6 eggs, divided

1 t. vanilla extract
4 t. baking powder
4 to 5 c. all-purpose flour

Cream butter until fluffy, about 15 minutes; gradually add sugar,
blending another 15 minutes. Add 4 eggs, one at a time, mixing
well after each addition; blend in vanilla and baking powder.
Gradually mix in flour until a stiff dough forms; roll dough into
walnut-size balls. Roll each ball into an 8-inch rope; fold in half
and twist 2 to 3 times. Place on aluminum foil-lined baking
sheets; set aside. Beat remaining eggs; brush onto each twist. Bake
at 350 degrees for 15 to 20 minutes. Makes about 5 dozen.

*Resist the urge to nibble on broken
cookies...they make tasty toppings
sprinkled on a dish of ice cream!*

That's the Way the Cookie Crumbles

Crème De Menthe Cookies

Jennifer Canfield
Davenport, IA

This is the perfect combination of mint and chocolate...all wrapped up in a soft, chewy cookie!

3/4 c. butter, softened
1-1/2 c. brown sugar, packed
2 T. water
2 c. chocolate chips
2 eggs

2-1/2 c. all-purpose flour
1-1/4 t. baking soda
3 4.67-oz. boxes crème de
   menthe thins, halved

Heat first 3 ingredients until sugar is dissolved; remove from heat. Stir in chocolate chips until melted; cool 10 minutes. Blend in eggs; set aside. In another mixing bowl, combine flour and baking soda; add to chocolate mixture, mixing well. Cover with plastic wrap; chill one hour. Roll dough into walnut-size balls; bake on ungreased baking sheets at 350 degrees for 8 to 9 minutes. Remove from oven and immediately place a mint wafer half on top of each ball. Spread like frosting when melted. Makes 3 dozen.

Simple shipping tags can become gift tags in a snap...just glue on a vintage sticker, buttons or family photo!

No-Bake Cookies

Lisa Wright
Garland, ME

No get-together is complete without these all-time favorites!

1/2 c. butter, softened
1/4 t. salt
1/2 c. milk
2 c. sugar
1/3 c. baking cocoa

3/4 c. creamy peanut butter
3 c. quick-cooking oats,
   uncooked
1 t. vanilla extract

Combine first 5 ingredients in a saucepan; boil for one to 2 minutes, stirring constantly. Remove from heat; stir in remaining ingredients. Drop by tablespoonfuls onto wax paper; cool. Makes about 4 dozen.

Cupboard Cookies

Toni McDonald
Jenison, MI

No one will guess the secret ingredient!

1 c. shortening
1 c. sugar
1 c. brown sugar, packed
1 c. potato chips, crushed
2 eggs

1 c. chopped walnuts
2 c. all-purpose flour
1 t. baking soda
1 t. salt

Combine all ingredients together in the order listed; mix well. Drop by tablespoonfuls onto ungreased baking sheets; bake at 325 degrees for 10 minutes. Makes about 3 dozen.

Cheer on your team with letter-shaped iced butter cookies outlined with colored sugar!

That's the Way the Cookie Crumbles

White Chocolate-Cranberry Cookies

Shawna Brock
Eglin AFB, FL

Dried cranberries have a surprisingly sweet taste and when paired with white chocolate will make these cookies a new favorite.

3/4 c. sugar
1/2 c. brown sugar, packed
1 c. sweetened, dried
　cranberries
1/2 c. white chocolate chips
1-3/4 c. all-purpose flour

1 t. baking powder
1/2 t. baking soda
1/2 c. butter, softened
1 egg, beaten
1 t. vanilla extract

Combine first 7 ingredients in a large mixing bowl; blend in remaining ingredients. Shape into walnut-size balls; place 2 inches apart on an ungreased baking sheet. Bake at 375 degrees for 13 to 15 minutes or until golden. Makes about 2-1/2 dozen.

A quick & easy cookie decorating tip: add chocolate, peanut butter or raspberry chips to a plastic zipping bag, seal and microwave until chips are melted. Then just snip off one small corner and pipe designs onto cooled cookies.

Snickerdoodles

Delores Berg
Selah, WA

An old-fashioned favorite that no one will pass up!

1-1/4 c. butter, softened
2-1/2 c. sugar, divided
2 eggs
1-1/2 t. vanilla extract
1/2 t. lemon extract
4-1/2 c. all-purpose flour

2 t. baking powder
1 t. baking soda
3/4 t. salt
1 c. buttermilk
2 T. cinnamon

Cream butter and 2 cups sugar; add eggs, one at a time, mixing well after each addition. Blend in extracts; set aside. In another mixing bowl, combine flour, baking powder, baking soda and salt; add alternately to sugar mixture with buttermilk. Cover and chill dough for 4 hours; shape quarter-cup measures of dough into balls. Roll in remaining sugar and cinnamon mixture; gently press balls 1/2-inch thick. Place 5 or 6 on each ungreased baking sheet; bake at 375 degrees for 15 minutes. Makes about 3 dozen.

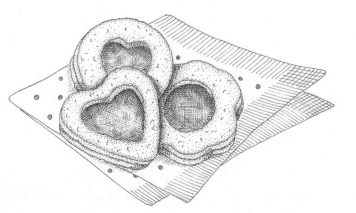

Clever invitations..."write" the time & date of your get-together in frosting on a nice big cookie, and then make the rounds with your special delivery!

That's the Way the Cookie Crumbles

Brown Sugar & Honey Cut-Outs

*Candy Hannigan
Monument, CO*

Enjoy these spicy cookies with a tall glass of milk...perfect!

1-1/2 c. butter, softened
1-1/2 c. brown sugar, packed
1 c. honey
1 egg
5-3/4 c. all-purpose flour

2 t. cinnamon
1 t. baking powder
1 t. baking soda
1 t. ground ginger
1 T. orange zest

Cream butter and sugar until fluffy; blend in honey and egg. In another mixing bowl, combine remaining ingredients; add to sugar mixture. Chill 2 or more hours. Roll out dough on a lightly floured surface to 1/8-inch thick; cut into desired shapes with cookie cutters. Bake on greased baking sheets at 350 degrees for 8 to 10 minutes; frost with either Chocolate or Decorator Frosting when cool. Makes 5 dozen.

Chocolate Frosting:

2 c. semi-sweet chocolate
chips, melted

2/3 c. sour cream

Combine warm chocolate chips with sour cream; stir until blended and smooth.

Decorator Frosting:

1 T. butter, softened
2 c. powdered sugar
1/2 t. almond extract

1-1/2 t. meringue powder
1 to 2 T. milk
paste food coloring

Blend all ingredients until smooth and creamy; divide into separate bowls and tint with color. Pipe designs using a pastry bag and decorating tips.

Old-Fashioned Lemon Cookies

Carol Hickman
Kingsport, TN

A tasty butter cookie with a hint of lemon.

1 c. butter, softened
1 c. sugar
2 egg yolks
1 t. lemon zest

1-1/2 c. all-purpose flour
1 c. cornmeal
Garnish: sugar

Cream butter and sugar; mix in egg yolks. Stir in lemon zest, flour and cornmeal; pat dough into a disk. Wrap in plastic wrap; refrigerate 3 to 4 hours. Roll out dough on a lightly floured surface to 1/8-inch thickness; cut into desired shapes using cookie cutters. Place on ungreased baking sheets; sprinkle with sugar. Bake at 350 degrees for 8 to 10 minutes or until edges are golden brown. Makes 3 dozen.

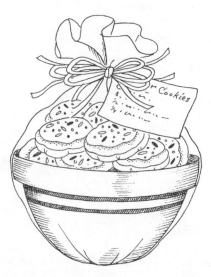

A vintage ornament box, lined with tissue paper and filled with cookies, is a terrific way to wish neighbors a Merry Christmas!

That's the Way the Cookie Crumbles

You-Name-It Cookies

Suzanne Killmon
Wallops Island, VA

Whoever chooses the cake mix flavor gets to name the cookies. We might have Sis' Strawberry Sweeties or Ma's Mega Lemon Snappers.

18-1/2 oz. pkg. cake mix
1 egg, beaten
8-oz. container frozen whipped
   topping, thawed

2 to 3 c. powdered sugar

Combine cake mix and egg; blend in whipped topping. Drop by teaspoonfuls into powdered sugar; coat completely. Place on ungreased baking sheets; bake at 350 degrees for 8 to 10 minutes. Cool on baking sheets. Makes 3 dozen.

Pudding No-Bakes

Vickie Chalfant
Mc Louth, KS

Use your favorite flavor of pudding in this recipe, then the next time you make them, try another flavor...the kids will love 'em!

3/4 c. evaporated milk
2 c. sugar
3/4 c. margarine
3-1/2 c. quick-cooking oats,
   uncooked

3-1/2 oz. pkg. instant pudding
mix

Combine milk, sugar and margarine in a heavy saucepan; bring to a boil. Remove from heat; add oats and pudding mix. Drop by tablespoonfuls onto wax paper; let cool. Makes 2 dozen.

Grammy's Chocolate Cookies

K. Peterson
Des Moines, IA

There's nothing like a day spent baking with grandchildren...it makes the sweetest memories.

2 c. all-purpose flour
3/4 c. baking cocoa
1 t. baking soda
1/2 t. salt

1-1/4 c. butter, softened
2-1/2 c. sugar, divided
2 eggs
2 t. vanilla extract

Sift flour, cocoa, baking soda and salt together; set aside. Blend butter, 2 cups sugar and eggs until light and fluffy, about 2 minutes; add vanilla. Gradually add dry ingredients to butter mixture; blend well. Cover dough with plastic wrap; chill one hour. Roll dough into one-inch balls; dip tops into remaining sugar. Place on lightly greased baking sheets about 1-1/2 inches apart; bake at 350 degrees for 8 minutes. Cool on baking sheets for 5 minutes before transferring to a wire rack to cool. Makes about 8 dozen.

Give a new co-worker a basket filled with freshly baked cookies...it's a sure way for them to meet and greet new friends.

That's the Way the Cookie Crumbles

Sour Cream Drop Cookies

Kathleen Souza
Acushnet, MA

For a slightly different taste, substitute golden raisins or sweetened, dried cranberries for raisins...just as yummy.

1/2 c. shortening
1-1/2 c. sugar
2 eggs, beaten
3 c. all-purpose flour
1 t. baking powder

1/2 t. baking soda
1/2 t. salt
3/4 c. sour cream
1 t. vanilla extract
15-oz. pkg. raisins

Cream shortening and sugar; gradually blend in eggs. In another mixing bowl, combine dry ingredients; add alternately with sour cream to sugar mixture. Blend in vanilla; drop by tablespoonfuls onto ungreased baking sheets. Place 3 raisins on each cookie; bake at 375 degrees for 10 to 12 minutes. Makes 2 to 3 dozen.

An old-fashioned, tin lunch box is just the right size to use as a cookie decorating kit. Cookie cutters, jimmies, colored sugars and sprinkles will fit nicely inside and everything will be right at your fingertips when it's cookie-baking time!

Best-Ever Coconut Cookies

Kathy Shepherd
Christiansburg, VA

*The simplest and best cookie recipe I've ever tried...I'm
"required" to bring them to every gathering!*

18-1/2 oz. pkg. yellow
   cake mix
1/2 c. oil
1/4 c. water

1 egg
1 t. coconut flavoring
8-oz. pkg. flaked coconut

Combine all ingredients except coconut together in a large mixing
bowl; blend well. Gradually stir in coconut; mix well. Drop by
tablespoonfuls onto ungreased baking sheets; bake at 350 degrees
for 10 minutes. Cool; store in an airtight container. Makes 4 to
5 dozen.

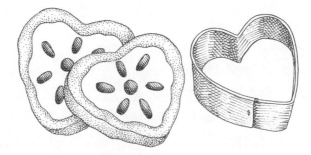

*Sprinkle powdered sugar on the work surface when
rolling out cookie dough...so much tastier than
using flour and it works just as well!*

Peppernuts

Flo Burtnett
Gage, OK

Youngsters in Germany sneak a clean plate from the cupboard to place on the kitchen table before snuggling into bed on Christmas Eve. The next morning, the plates are loaded with goodies...among them, small, spicy cookies called peppernuts!

1 c. all-purpose flour
1/4 t. baking soda
1/4 t. salt
1 t. cinnamon
1/4 t. ground cloves
1/4 t. allspice
1/4 t. pepper

1/4 c. candied citron, chopped
1/4 c. candied orange peel, chopped
3 T. butter, softened
1 c. powdered sugar
1 egg, beaten

Combine first 7 ingredients together in a medium-size bowl; stir in citron and orange peel. In a large mixing bowl, cream butter and powdered sugar together; add egg. Gradually blend in flour mixture; cover and refrigerate dough overnight. Roll 1/2 teaspoonfuls of dough into balls; place on greased baking sheets about 2 inches apart. Bake at 350 degrees for 10 to 12 minutes, or until lightly golden; cool on wire racks. Makes 4 to 5 dozen.

Once in a young lifetime one should be allowed to have as much sweetness as one can possibly hold.
-Judith Olney

Mémé's Molasses Cookies

Amie Forgeron-Wheeler
Torrance, CA

*This is my great-grandmother's recipe...handed
down through our family, it's always a favorite.*

3/4 c. shortening
1-1/2 c. sugar, divided
1 egg
4 T. molasses
2 c. all-purpose flour

2 t. baking soda
1 t. cinnamon
1/2 t. ground cloves
1 t. ground ginger

Blend shortening, one cup sugar, egg and molasses together until
fluffy; set aside. Combine flour, baking soda, cinnamon, cloves and
ginger together; gradually mix into molasses mixture. Cover and chill
dough for 30 minutes. Shape dough into walnut-size balls; roll in
remaining sugar. Place on ungreased baking sheets about 2 inches
apart; bake at 350 degrees for 10 minutes. Cool on baking sheet one
minute; remove to cooling rack. Makes about 4 dozen.

*Kitchen gadgets come in handy when decorating
cookies. Did you know you can squeeze dough
through a garlic press to make "hair" for a sweet
gingerbread girl?*

That's the Way the Cookie Crumbles

Cinnamon Chip Icebox Cookies

Christy Worley
Rural Retreat, VA

*Great for any get-together, this recipe makes
6 dozen sweet and spicy cinnamon cookies.*

1 c. butter, softened
2 c. sugar
2 eggs
1 t. vanilla extract

4 c. all-purpose flour
10-oz. pkg. cinnamon chips
1 c. chopped pecans

Cream butter and sugar together; add eggs and vanilla. Gradually mix in flour; fold in cinnamon chips and pecans. Divide dough into 3 portions; roll each portion into a 12-inch long log. Wrap in wax paper; refrigerate 8 hours. Slice each log into 24 slices; place on ungreased baking sheets. Bake at 350 degrees for 13 to 16 minutes; cool. Makes 6 dozen.

*Inspire a young baker with a cookie-making kit.
Fill a basket with all the basics...rolling pin,
favorite recipes, cookie cutters, sprinkles, measuring
spoons and cups. Top it off with a batch of
homemade cookies for them to nibble on!*

The Ultimate Chip Cookies

Cindy Griffin
Bloomfield, MO

Bursting with flavor, these will be an instant hit!

2-1/2 c. all-purpose flour
1 t. baking soda
1/2 t. salt
1 c. butter, softened
1 c. brown sugar, packed
1/2 c. sugar
2 eggs

1 T. vanilla extract
3/4 c. chocolate chips
3/4 c. white chocolate chips
3/4 c. peanut butter chips
3/4 c. candy-coated chocolate
　　mini-baking bits
1/2 c. chopped pecans

Combine flour, baking soda and salt; set aside. In a large mixing bowl, cream butter and sugars together until light and fluffy; blend in eggs and vanilla. Mix flour mixture into butter mixture; fold in chips, baking bits and pecans. Drop by tablespoonfuls 2 inches apart onto ungreased baking sheets; bake at 375 degrees for 10 to 12 minutes. Cool on baking sheets for 2 minutes; remove to wire racks to cool completely. Makes about 4 dozen.

Treats a busy mom would love anytime...spoon scoops of cookie dough onto baking sheets and freeze. After the dough is frozen, toss in a plastic zipping bag labeled with the cookie name and baking instructions.

That's the Way the Cookie Crumbles

Peanut Butter Cookies

Mitzi Kolp
New Berlin, WI

For an extra-special touch, use the bottom of a patterned juice glass to flatten out the dough balls...lovely!

1/4 c. butter-flavored
   shortening
1/4 c. butter
3/4 c. creamy peanut butter
1/2 c. sugar
1/2 c. brown sugar, packed

1 egg
1/2 t. baking powder
3/4 t. baking soda
1/4 t. salt
1-1/4 c. all-purpose flour

Blend first 6 ingredients together; set aside. Combine remaining ingredients; add to butter mixture. Cover and chill dough for about one hour. Roll into walnut-size balls; place on ungreased baking sheets about 3 inches apart. Flatten with a fork dipped in sugar; bake at 350 degrees for 10 to 12 minutes. Makes about 3 dozen.

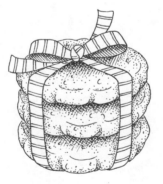

Nothing spoils the taste of peanut butter like unrequited love.
-Charlie Brown

Cookie Dough

Norma Baxter
Mishawaka, IN

Ideal for all the cookie dough lovers and all those cookie makers who are always chasing the eaters out of their dough!

1 c. butter, softened
1-1/2 c. brown sugar, packed
2 t. vanilla extract
1/2 t. salt

2 c. all-purpose flour
1 T. water
6-oz. pkg. mini chocolate chips

Cream butter and sugar together; add remaining ingredients, mixing well. Roll into bite-size balls; freeze until firm, about 30 minutes. Store in a plastic zipping bag in the freezer. Makes about 4 dozen.

When the kids come home from school, greet them with their favorite cookies. Served with a tall glass of milk...you'll be making memories to last a lifetime.

That's the Way the Cookie Crumbles

Chocolate Blossoms

Delinda Blakney
Bridgeview, IL

You can also top these favorites with chocolate stars or mini peanut butter cups.

1-3/4 c. all-purpose flour
1/2 c. sugar
1/2 c. brown sugar, packed
1 t. baking soda
1/2 t. salt
1/2 c. shortening

1/2 c. creamy peanut butter
2 T. milk
1 t. vanilla extract
1 egg
additional sugar for coating
48 milk chocolate drops

Combine all ingredients except chocolate drops and coating sugar; blend on low speed to form a stiff dough. Shape dough into one-inch balls; coat with sugar. Place 2 inches apart on ungreased baking sheets; bake at 375 degrees for 10 to 12 minutes. Remove from oven; immediately top each cookie with a chocolate drop, pressing down firmly. Makes about 4 dozen.

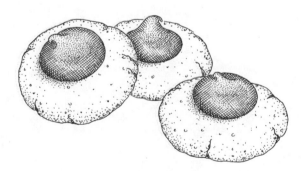

Tie a cookie gift tag on special gifts...so easy! Before baking cut-out cookies, make a hole in each with a straw and bake. Once cookies have cooled, raffia or ribbon will slip right through.

Pumpkin-Chocolate Chip Cookies

Stephanie Thys
Victor, IA

If you're like me and can't resist tossing chocolate chips in your pumpkin bread, then you'll love this cookie recipe!

1/2 c. margarine
1-1/2 c. sugar
1 egg
1 c. canned pumpkin
1 t. vanilla extract
2-1/2 c. all-purpose flour

1 t. baking powder
1/2 t. salt
1 t. nutmeg
1 t. cinnamon
6-oz. pkg. chocolate chips
Optional: chopped nuts

Cream margarine and sugar together; set aside. Combine egg, pumpkin and vanilla; blend into creamed mixture and set aside. Mix dry ingredients together; blend into pumpkin mixture. Fold in chocolate chips and nuts, if desired. Drop by tablespoonfuls onto lightly greased baking sheets; bake at 350 degrees until lightly golden, about 8 minutes. Makes about 3-1/2 dozen.

Health food may be good for the conscience, but Oreos taste a lot better.
-Robert Redford

That's the Way the Cookie Crumbles

Honey-Nut Cookies

Jean Marie DePerna
Ontario, NY

Mom was thrilled every time I made these cookies...and I always made them just for her.

2 c. all-purpose flour
1/2 t. salt
1 c. chilled butter, sliced
8-oz. pkg. cream cheese, sliced
1 c. nuts, ground

1/4 c. sugar
6 T. honey
1 t. butter, melted
1/2 t. cinnamon

Combine flour and salt; cut in chilled butter and cream cheese using a pastry cutter or 2 forks. Divide dough into quarters; wrap each individually in plastic wrap. Chill at least one hour. To prepare filling, mix nuts and sugar together; stir in honey, melted butter and cinnamon. Set aside. Roll out chilled dough to 1/2-inch thickness; cut into 2-inch circles using a glass or biscuit cutter. Spoon one teaspoonful filling into middle of each circle; wet edge of circle with water. Place another circle on top; press edges with a fork to seal. Bake on lightly greased baking sheets at 325 degrees for 22 to 25 minutes or until golden. Cool on wire racks. Makes 2 to 3 dozen.

The trick to keeping a powdered sugar garnish on the cookies? Dust the tops of cookies while they're still warm.

Charleston Pecan Sandies

Terry Stewart
Cayce, SC

Enjoy with a cup of chamomile tea...perfect together.

4 c. all-purpose flour
2 c. butter, softened
4 c. chopped pecans
8 T. sugar

1/2 t. salt
4 t. vanilla extract
2 c. powdered sugar

Combine first 6 ingredients together; cover and refrigerate until firm. Roll into 1/2-inch balls; flatten slightly. Place on ungreased baking sheets; bake at 375 degrees for 15 to 20 minutes. Sprinkle powdered sugar over the tops. Makes about 6 dozen.

Little girls will love cookie necklaces...just thread mini sugar-dusted cookies on wax-covered thread for an edible treat that's extra-special!

That's the Way the Cookie Crumbles

Nut Roll Cookies

SallyAnn Cortese
Sewickley, PA

Even though this is the same recipe my mother-in-law shared with me, my husband says my cookies are better than hers!

1 pkg. active dry yeast
1 c. milk, warmed
2 c. margarine
6 c. all-purpose flour

3 T. sugar
3 eggs, unbeaten
Garnish: powdered sugar

Sprinkle yeast in warm milk; set aside. Combine margarine, flour and sugar together with a pastry cutter; stir in yeast mixture. Blend in eggs; set aside. Divide dough into 10 equal portions; roll out each section into a circle on a lightly floured and sugared surface. Cut into 12 wedges; spread with a thin layer of filling. Roll up crescent-roll style; place on ungreased baking sheets. Bake at 450 degrees for about 6 minutes or until slightly golden. Cool; sprinkle with powdered sugar. Makes 10 dozen.

Filling:

4 c. English walnuts, ground
1 c. sugar

1 to 2 T. milk or water

Combine nuts and sugar together; stir in enough milk or water to moisten and make desired spreading consistency.

Italian Cookies

Suzanne Morell
Valley Springs, CA

These light, sweet cookies disappear quickly at
family gatherings and get-togethers!

6 c. all-purpose flour
2 T. baking powder
1/2 t. salt
3 eggs
1-1/2 c. sugar

2/3 c. milk
1 T. vanilla extract
1/2 lb. shortening, melted
    and cooled
Garnish: non-pareils

Combine first 3 ingredients in a large mixing bowl; set aside. Blend eggs, sugar, milk and vanilla together; mix in cooled shortening. Stir into flour mixture; drop by tablespoonfuls onto ungreased baking sheets. Bake at 450 degrees for 8 to 10 minutes or until golden brown. Cool; frost and dip in non-pareils. Makes about 6 dozen.

Frosting:

4 c. powdered sugar
1/4 c. milk

1/2 c. butter, softened
2 t. vanilla extract

Combine all ingredients in a large mixing bowl; blend on low speed for one minute. Increase speed to medium; blend until fluffy, about 2 minutes.

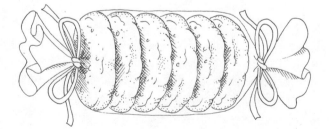

That's the Way the Cookie Crumbles

Spritz

Juanita Williams
Jacksonville, OR

Many, many good memories come with this recipe. Taken from one of Mom's old Swedish cookbooks, it makes great cookies every time.

1 c. butter	1/2 t. almond extract
1/2 c. sugar	2 c. all-purpose flour
1 egg yolk	1/4 t. salt

Cream butter and sugar together; add egg yolk and extract. In another mixing bowl, sift flour and salt; add to sugar mixture. Press dough through a cookie press, using a small star disk, onto ungreased baking sheets in alphabet letter shapes. Bake at 350 degrees for 8 to 10 minutes or until golden. Makes 5 to 6 dozen.

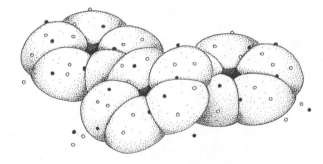

Give spritz cookies a new twist...shape the dough into rings and decorate with sprinkles...sweet wreaths to hang on a Christmas tree!

Frosted Orange Cookies

Laura Lett
Gooseberry Patch

*A light tasting cookie that is also eye-catching
at baby or wedding showers.*

1 c. shortening
1-1/2 c. sugar
2 eggs
1/3 c. orange juice, strained
1 T. orange zest
4 c. all-purpose flour

1/8 t. salt
1 t. baking soda
4 t. baking powder
1 c. less 1 T. milk
2 T. lemon juice

Cream shortening; blend in sugar and eggs. Add orange juice and zest; set aside. Sift flour, salt, baking soda and baking powder together 3 times; set aside. Combine milk and lemon juice together; add to creamed mixture alternately with flour mixture. Drop by teaspoonfuls onto greased and floured baking sheets; bake at 350 degrees for 9 to 10 minutes. Frost while still warm. Makes about 5 dozen.

Frosting:

1-lb. pkg. powdered sugar
2 to 4 T. orange juice

1 T. orange zest

Blend ingredients together until creamy; adjust orange juice amount to achieve desired spreading consistency.

That's the Way the Cookie Crumbles

Sugared Pecan Cookies

Kathy McLaren
Visalia, CA

These snowy cookies look beautiful layered in a gift box lined with red tissue paper...what a sweet surprise.

1/2 c. butter, softened	1 T. sugar
1/2 c. cream cheese, softened	1/8 t. salt
1 t. vanilla extract	1 c. pecans, ground
1-3/4 c. all-purpose flour	1 c. powdered sugar

Cream butter and cream cheese together; blend in vanilla and set aside. Combine flour, sugar and salt; gradually blend into creamed mixture. Stir in pecans; shape each tablespoonful of dough into a 2-inch log. Place 2 inches apart on ungreased baking sheets; bake at 375 degrees for 12 to 14 minutes. Roll warm cookies in powdered sugar; cool on wire racks. Makes 2 dozen.

Spoon cookie frosting into individual muffin tins before tinting...an easy way to keep the colors separated!

Beacon Hill Cookies

Julie Cavender
Riverside, CA

Given to me by my mother, this recipe has always been one of my very favorites. We always make them at Christmastime, but trust me, they're great any time of year!

2 egg whites
1/4 t. salt
1/2 c. sugar
1/2 t. vanilla extract

1/2 t. vinegar
6-oz. pkg. chocolate chips,
   melted
3/4 c. chopped walnuts

Beat egg whites and salt until foamy; gradually blend in sugar. Continue beating until stiff peaks form; mix in vanilla and vinegar. Fold melted chocolate and nuts into egg whites; drop by teaspoonfuls onto greased baking sheets. Bake at 350 degrees for 10 minutes or until top becomes puffy and cracked. Cool. Makes about 3 dozen.

What cookies and milk have going for them
is that they speak of home...
-Bob Sloan

That's the Way the Cookie Crumbles

Lemon-Cream Cheese Cookies

Melissa Ing
Glastonbury, CT

These cut-out cookies are so good, they don't even need frosting!

1 c. butter, softened
8-oz. pkg. cream cheese,
   softened
1 c. sugar
5 T. lemon juice
1 t. lemon zest

4-1/2 c. all-purpose flour
1 T. cinnamon
1/2 t. ground cloves
1/4 t. nutmeg
1/8 t. salt

Mix butter, cream cheese and sugar together; add lemon juice and zest. In a separate bowl, combine flour and remaining spices; add to butter mixture, mixing well. Cover and refrigerate for at least one hour; roll out dough to 1/4-inch thickness. Cut into desired shapes using cookie cutters; bake at 325 degrees for approximately 10 minutes or until edges are light golden. Makes about 4 dozen.

Make a sweet cookie bouquet using soft sugar cookies. Slip a lollipop stick into baked and decorated cookies, then tuck in a flower pot filled with florist's foam. A surprise anyone will love!

Florentines

Michelle Doherty
Kansas City, MO

Thin lacy cookies topped with rich chocolate.

1 c. blanched almonds, finely
  chopped
1/2 c. mixed candied fruits,
  finely chopped
1/3 c. butter
1/3 c. milk

1/4 c. sugar
2 T. honey
1/4 to 1/2 c. all-purpose flour
1 c. semi-sweet chocolate chips
2 T. shortening

Combine almonds and fruits; set aside. Add butter, milk, sugar and
honey to a saucepan; bring to a rolling boil, stirring occasionally.
Remove from heat; stir in almond and fruit mixture. Stir in flour
until thickened; drop by level teaspoonfuls 3 inches apart onto
greased and floured baking sheets with no more than 6 cookies per
sheet. Spread dough into 3-inch circles using the back of a spoon;
bake at 350 degrees for 8 to 10 minutes. Remove from oven; let
stand one minute. Carefully remove with spatula to wax paper; cool
completely. Melt chocolate chips with shortening in a double boiler;
spread one teaspoonful on bottom of each cookie. When chocolate is
almost set; draw wavy lines through chocolate with tines of a fork.
Store in refrigerator. Makes 2 to 3 dozen.

*Did you know…if you tuck a wet paper towel in
the bottom of a drinking glass and then set a
piping bag filled with icing inside, it keeps
the tips from drying out?*

That's the Way the Cookie Crumbles

Grandma Grover's Hermits

Nancy Campbell
Bellingham, WA

It was an extra-special treat the first time I was invited to Grandma's to watch her mix, roll and cut out these cookies. The memories of that wonderful day remain with me still.

1-1/2 c. brown sugar, packed
2/3 c. shortening
2 eggs, beaten
1 c. raisins
2 T. milk

1 t. baking soda
1 t. cinnamon
1/2 t. ground cloves
1/8 t. nutmeg
2-1/4 c. all-purpose flour

Cream brown sugar and shortening together; add eggs, blending well. Mix in raisins and milk; set aside. In a separate bowl combine all dry ingredients; mix thoroughly. Stir into creamed mixture; roll half of the dough on a floured surface. Cut into large irregular pieces and place on ungreased baking sheets; repeat for remaining dough. Bake at 400 degrees until golden brown, about 10 minutes. Cool on wire racks. Makes 3 to 4 dozen.

A cookie exchange is a great way to enjoy lots of different cookies! Invite 12 friends to bring a dozen of their favorite cookies for swapping. (Everyone should bring a different type of cookie.) After choosing cookies from everyone's plate, you'll each go home with 12 different yummy cookies!

Sugared Marble Cookies

Liz Wilmot
Honeoye Falls, NY

A melt-in-your-mouth cookie!

1 c. shortening
1 c. sugar
1-1/4 t. vanilla extract
1-1/4 t. almond extract
1 egg
2 c. all-purpose flour

1/2 t. salt
1/2 t. baking soda
1/2 t. cream of tartar
1-oz. sq. baking chocolate,
    melted

Cream shortening and sugar; add extracts and egg, blending until fluffy. In another mixing bowl, sift together dry ingredients; add to creamed mixture. Drizzle chocolate over dough, a little at a time, and cut it in with a knife. Do not stir. Form dough into one-inch balls and place on ungreased baking sheets; flatten slightly with bottom of drinking glass dipped in sugar. Bake at 400 degrees for 8 to 10 minutes or until edges are golden. Makes about 3 dozen.

Short on time? Spread cookie dough in a 13"x9" baking pan and make bar cookies instead of individual drop cookies...they'll be just as delicious!

That's the Way the Cookie Crumbles

Chocolate-Coconut Chews

Elaine Woelich
Mendham, NJ

A snap to make and the ingredients are almost always on hand.

1 c. brown sugar, packed
1 c. sugar
1 c. oil
1 c. margarine, softened
1 egg
2 t. vanilla extract
1 c. flaked coconut
1 t. salt

1 t. baking soda
1 t. cream of tartar
1 c. quick-cooking oats,
   uncooked
3-1/2 c. all-purpose flour
1 c. crispy rice cereal
8-oz. pkg. chocolate chips

Mix all ingredients together in the order listed. Stir with spoon; mix well. Shape dough into one-inch balls; flatten slightly with the bottom of a glass that has been dipped in sugar. Bake for 12 to 15 minutes at 350 degrees on a greased baking sheet. Makes 5 to 6 dozen.

Sparkly sanding sugar gives cookies a pretty snow-dusted look. Sprinkle on while the icing is still wet, wait 5 minutes, then gently shake off any excess.

Mini Taffy-Apple Cookies

Delinda Blakney
Bridgeview, IL

These look just like mini apples!

1 c. plus 2 T. butter
1/2 c. powdered sugar
2 egg yolks
3 c. all-purpose flour

14-oz. pkg. caramels,
   unwrapped
3/4 c. milk
1 c. nuts, ground

Combine butter, powdered sugar, egg yolks and flour; mix well. Shape dough into one-inch balls; place one inch apart on ungreased baking sheets. Bake at 375 degrees for 12 to 15 minutes; cool completely. Place a toothpick cut in half into the center of each ball; set aside. In a double boiler, combine caramels and milk; heat until melted, stirring constantly. Dip each cookie ball into caramel mixture; let drip and then dip into ground nuts. Place in mini baking cups to set. Makes about 100.

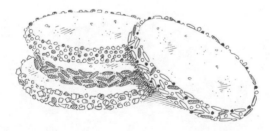

Craving something that's both sweet & salty?
Make a favorite sugar cookie recipe,
shape dough into one-inch balls, roll in
crushed pretzels and bake...yummy!

That's the Way the Cookie Crumbles

Chocolate Thumbprint Cookies

Ann Fehr
Trappe, PA

A chocolatey twist to an old favorite.

1/2 c. plus 1 t. butter, softened
   and divided
1 c. sugar, divided
1 egg yolk
2 T. plus 2 t. milk, divided
2-1/4 t. vanilla extract, divided

1 c. all-purpose flour
1/3 c. baking cocoa
1/4 t. salt
1/2 c. powdered sugar
24 milk chocolate drops

In a small mixing bowl, cream 1/2 cup butter, 2/3 cup sugar, egg yolk, 2 tablespoons milk and 2 tablespoons vanilla together until light and fluffy; set aside. Combine flour, cocoa and salt; add to butter mixture, beating until well blended. Refrigerate dough at least one hour; shape into one-inch balls. Roll in remaining sugar; place on lightly greased baking sheets. Press thumb gently into center of each ball; bake at 350 degrees for 10 to 12 minutes. While baking, blend together powdered sugar, remaining butter, milk and vanilla. When cookies are done baking, spoon 1/4 teaspoon filling into each thumbprint; gently press chocolate drop on top of filling. Remove from baking sheets; cool completely on wire rack. Makes 2 dozen.

Even the smallest kids can lend a hand in the kitchen...little thumbs make the sweetest indents for thumbprint cookies!

43

Ginger Meringue Cookies

Tami Bowman
Gooseberry Patch

Deliciously crisp.

2 egg whites
1/8 t. cream of tartar
1/3 c. sugar

1 T. crystallized ginger, grated
1/4 t. almond extract

Beat egg whites and cream of tartar on high speed until soft peaks form; gradually add sugar, blending constantly until stiff peaks form. Fold in ginger and almond extract; drop by tablespoonfuls onto a parchment-lined baking sheet. Bake at 300 degrees for 40 minutes or until dry and crisp; turn oven off, do not remove meringues or open oven door for at least 2 hours. Remove from parchment; store meringues in an airtight container. Makes about 2 dozen.

Take time to invite a friend over for afternoon tea. Serve freshly baked cookies with a steaming pot of herbal tea and spend time just catching up.

Easy As Pie

Glazed Apple-Cream Pie

Elizabeth Andrus
Gooseberry Patch

In days gone by, a meal was never complete without the crowning touch of dessert. It was the moment to heap praise on the cook who was known for her special recipe...a recipe often not shared!

1/2 c. sugar	9-inch pie crust, baked
1/2 c. plus 2 T. milk, divided	9-inch pie crust, unbaked
1/2 c. whipping cream	2 Granny Smith apples, cored,
1/4 c. butter, softened	peeled and sliced
2 T. cornstarch	1 T. all-purpose flour
1 t. vanilla extract	1 t. cinnamon

Heat sugar, 1/2 cup milk, cream and butter in a medium saucepan over low heat until butter is melted; while heating, combine remaining milk and cornstarch. Add to saucepan; heat until smooth, about 7 minutes. Remove from heat; add vanilla. Cool; pour into bottom baked crust. In a separate mixing bowl, combine apples, flour and cinnamon; sprinkle over filling. Top with remaining unbaked crust; flute edges. Vent top crust; cover edges with aluminum foil. Bake at 400 degrees for 45 to 50 minutes. Spread topping on warm pie; refrigerate 1-1/2 hours before serving. Makes 8 servings.

Topping:

1/2 c. powdered sugar	1/4 t. vanilla extract
1 T. milk	1 T. butter

Cream ingredients until smooth.

My tongue is smiling!
-Abigail Trillain

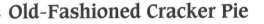

Easy As Pie!

Old-Fashioned Cracker Pie

Crystal Burchfield
Alabaster, AL

An old-fashioned Southern favorite. The secret to this pie is to refrigerate overnight before serving.

3 egg whites
1/2 t. cream of tartar
1 c. sugar
1 c. chopped pecans
20 saltine crackers, crushed

8-oz. can crushed pineapple, drained
8-oz. container frozen whipped topping, thawed

Beat egg whites and cream of tartar together until stiff peaks form. Add sugar while beating until mixture becomes thick and glossy; fold in pecans and crackers. Spread into a buttered 9" glass pie pan; bake at 325 degrees for 20 to 25 minutes or until golden. Cool completely. In a mixing bowl, blend pineapple and whipped topping together; spread over pie. Refrigerate overnight before serving. Makes 8 servings.

Make a sweet treat while waiting for the pie to bake. Twist scraps of remaining pie dough and roll in a mixture of cinnamon & sugar. Bake at 350 degrees for 10 minutes...so quick & easy!

Coffee-Nut Torte

Gail Foster
Leavittsburg, OH

A delight for any coffee lover!

6 eggs, separated
2 c. sugar
1 t. vanilla extract
1 c. coffee, cold and divided

1 c. walnuts, ground
2 c. all-purpose flour
3 t. baking powder

Cream egg yolks, sugar, vanilla and 1/4 cup coffee together; beat until thick. In a separate mixing bowl, combine walnuts, flour and baking powder together; add to egg mixture alternately with remaining coffee. Beat egg whites until stiff peak forms; fold into coffee mixture. Pour into 2 greased, round, 9" baking pans. Bake at 350 degrees for 25 minutes. Cool, then frost. Makes 16 servings.

Frosting:

1/2 c. brown sugar, packed
1/4 c. milk
3 T. all-purpose flour
water

1 t. vanilla extract
1/2 t. maple flavoring
1 c. butter, softened
2 c. powdered sugar

Combine brown sugar, milk and flour in a saucepan; add enough water to form a paste. Stir in vanilla and maple flavoring; heat until thickened and then set aside to cool. In another mixing bowl, cream butter; gradually mix in powdered sugar, blending well. Add cooled mixture; blend until light and fluffy.

Make dessert a grand finale...serve it on your prettiest china!

Easy As Pie!

Chocolate-Butterscotch Pie

Kathy Grashoff
Fort Wayne, IN

This classic is a favorite from the 1930's.

3/4 c. brown sugar, packed
1/3 c. all-purpose flour
1/2 t. salt
2-1/2 c. milk
6 T. chocolate syrup

2 egg yolks, beaten
2 T. butter
1/2 t. vanilla extract
9-inch pie crust, baked
Garnish: whipped topping

Thoroughly combine sugar, flour and salt; stir in milk, chocolate syrup and egg yolks. Pour into a saucepan over medium heat until thick; stir constantly. Remove from heat; blend in butter and vanilla. Pour into pie crust; cool to room temperature. Refrigerate until firm; serve with a dollop of whipped topping. Makes 8 servings.

Stir up sweet memories...look through Grandma's recipe box and rediscover a long-forgotten favorite dessert recipe to share.

Gold Pie

Kathy McLaren
Visalia, CA

*This pie gets its name from the beautiful golden color
the crust turns as it bakes to perfection.*

6 T. all-purpose flour
6 T. butter, melted
2 c. sugar, divided
4 eggs, separated

1-1/2 c. milk
zest of one lemon
2 T. lemon juice
Garnish: powdered sugar

Combine flour, butter and 1-1/2 cups sugar in a large mixing bowl;
set aside. Beat egg yolks; add to sugar mixture. Mix in milk, lemon
zest and lemon juice; set aside. In another bowl, beat egg whites until
stiff; gradually add remaining sugar, blending well. Fold into batter;
pour into a greased, 2-quart baking dish. Place in a shallow pan of
hot water; bake at 350 degrees for 55 to 60 minutes or until lightly
golden. Serve warm or chilled; dust with powdered sugar before
serving. Makes 8 to 10 servings.

The little things that make life sweet
Are worth their weight in gold;
They can't be bought at any price,
And neither are they sold.
-Unknown

Easy As Pie!

Raspberry-Cheese Pie

Rita Miller
Aberdeen, MD

Sweet berries topped with a chocolatey glaze...delicious!

2 3-oz. pkgs. cream cheese,
   softened
14-oz. can sweetened
   condensed milk
1 egg
3 T. lemon juice

1 t. vanilla extract
1 c. raspberries
8-inch chocolate cookie pie crust
2 1-oz. sqs. semi-sweet baking
   chocolate
1/4 c. whipping cream

Blend cream cheese until light and fluffy; gradually add condensed milk. Mix in egg, lemon juice and vanilla; blend well. Arrange berries on bottom of pie crust; pour cream cheese mixture over berries. Bake at 350 degrees for 30 to 35 minutes or until set; cool completely. Melt chocolate chips with whipping cream in a double boiler; stir until thick and smooth. Spread over top of pie; refrigerate until serving. Makes 8 servings.

For a new twist, host a pie party and invite everyone to bring their best-loved pie to share. Bring home a brand new recipe...it just might become a favorite!

Glazed Strawberry Tart

Jo Ann

Really show off this tart for special occasions...drizzle with melted chocolate or dust with powdered sugar!

1-1/2 c. all-purpose flour
1/2 c. almonds, ground
1/3 c. sugar
1/2 t. salt
6 T. chilled butter, sliced
1 egg

1 t. almond extract
3/4 c. strawberry jam
1 t. lemon juice
2 pts. strawberries, hulled
   and halved
Garnish: whipped topping

Stir flour, almonds, sugar and salt together in a large mixing bowl; cut butter into mixture until coarse crumbs form. In another bowl, whisk egg and almond extract together; stir into flour mixture until dough forms. Shape into a flattened ball; wrap in plastic wrap and refrigerate overnight. Grease and flour a baking sheet; place dough in center. Pat into a 10-inch circle; form a 3/4-inch high rim around the outside edge. Prick bottom of dough with a fork; bake at 350 degrees for 25 minutes or until golden. Cool 10 minutes on baking sheet on wire rack; transfer crust to rack to cool completely. Melt jam with lemon juice in a small saucepan over low heat until spreadable; spread 1/2 cup jam mixture over crust. Arrange berry slices on top, cut-sides down; brush with remaining jam mixture. Serve with whipped topping. Makes 8 servings.

Look for vintage pie tins, servers and cake plates at flea markets...add them to your own collection or make them part of the gift when sharing a favorite sweet treat.

Easy As Pie!

Classic Cheesecake

Liz Moore
Plano, TX

So versatile...top it with blueberries, cherries or kiwi slices.

1-1/4 c. graham cracker crumbs
1/4 c. sugar
1 t. cinnamon

1/4 c. butter, melted
1 pt. strawberries, hulled
    and sliced

Mix ingredients, except strawberries, together in a small mixing bowl; press firmly into the bottom of a lightly greased, 9" springform pan. Pour filling onto crust; bake at 300 degrees for one hour and 15 minutes. Cover and refrigerate 4 hours before serving. Top with strawberries. Makes 12 servings.

Filling:

4 8-oz. pkgs. cream cheese,
    softened
1 c. sugar

4 eggs
2 t. lemon juice
1 t. vanilla extract

Blend cream cheese until creamy; gradually add sugar, blending well. Add eggs, one at a time, mixing well after each addition; stir in lemon juice and vanilla.

Dress up plain cheesecake in a jiffy...drizzle slices with warm, raspberry preserves.

Coconut-Caramel Crunch Pie

Valarie Dennard
Palatka, FL

Toasted coconut and pecans give this tasty pie its delicious crunch.

1/4 c. butter
1/2 c. chopped pecans
7-oz. pkg. flaked coconut
8-oz. pkg. cream cheese,
  softened
14-oz. can sweetened
  condensed milk

16-oz. container frozen whipped
  topping, thawed
2 9-inch deep-dish pie crusts,
  baked
Garnish: caramel ice cream
  topping

Melt butter in a 10" skillet; add pecans and coconut, stirring
frequently, until coconut is golden. In a mixing bowl, blend cream
cheese and milk together; fold in whipped topping. Spread a quarter
of the mixture into each pie crust; drizzle caramel topping on top.
Sprinkle a quarter of the coconut and pecan mixture over each pie;
repeat layers. Cover; freeze until firm. Let stand 5 minutes at room
temperature before serving. Makes 16 servings.

*Give fruit pies an
extra burst of flavor!
When making a
favorite pie crust recipe,
instead of using ice water,
substitute the same amount
of berry-flavored
carbonated water.*

Easy As Pie!

Chocolate-Marshmallow Pie

Linda Taylor
Watha, NC

Tastes just like an old-fashioned Moon Pie!

2 c. mini marshmallows
2 c. plus 2 T. milk, divided
2-1/2 c. frozen whipped
    topping, thawed and divided
2 4-oz. pkgs. instant chocolate
    pudding mix

8-inch chocolate cookie pie crust
Garnish: vanilla wafers and
    chocolate syrup

Melt marshmallows with 2 tablespoons milk in a saucepan over low heat, stirring constantly. Remove from heat; cool. Fold in one cup whipped topping; refrigerate mixture while preparing remainder of pie. In a large mixing bowl, mix remaining milk with pudding; whisk for 2 minutes. Fold in remaining whipped topping; spoon into pie crust. Arrange layer of vanilla wafers on top; spread with chilled marshmallow mixture. Refrigerate 4 hours; drizzle with chocolate syrup before serving. Makes 8 servings.

Gently press mini cookie cutters on the top pastry of a two-crust pie, being careful not to go through the dough...little hearts and stars leave the prettiest patterns!

Lemonade-Ice Cream Pie

Cheryl Laufer
Chesterland, OH

Try substituting limeade or pink lemonade for a fresh new taste.

1/2 gal. vanilla ice cream or
　frozen yogurt, softened
12-oz. can frozen lemonade
　concentrate, thawed
16-oz. container frozen whipped
　topping, thawed and divided

2　9-inch graham cracker pie
　crusts, frozen
Garnish: lemon slices and mint
　sprigs

Mix ice cream or yogurt, lemonade and half of the whipped topping together; divide and spread equally into pie crusts. Spread with remaining whipped topping; freeze, uncovered, until firm. Cover with plastic wrap and freeze an additional 4 hours. Garnish with lemon slices and mint sprigs before serving. Makes 8 to 10 servings.

A terrific gift for the pie-lover in your life...a certificate for a Pie-of-the-Month Club! They'll love it when you deliver a yummy homemade pie each month.

Easy As Pie!

Strawberry-Yogurt Pie

Michelle Rooney
Gooseberry Patch

*A very easy-to-make, refreshing dessert I've made
for many years. My kids always loved it when
they were little and now, as grown-ups, they still do!*

2 8-oz. cartons strawberry
   yogurt
1/2 c. strawberries, hulled
   and crushed

8-oz. container frozen whipped
   topping, thawed
9-inch graham cracker pie crust

Combine yogurt and strawberries; mix well. Fold in whipped topping;
blend well. Spoon into crust; freeze 4 hours. Remove and place in
refrigerator for 30 minutes before serving. Makes 8 servings.

Pear Pie

Shirley Heinlein
Upper Arlington, OH

So quick to make, it's a favorite of our book club!

4 pears, cored, peeled and
   thinly sliced
3 T. frozen orange juice
   concentrate, thawed
9-inch pie crust, unbaked

1/2 c. sugar
1/8 t. salt
3/4 c. all-purpose flour
1/3 c. butter
2 t. cinnamon, divided

Toss pears and orange juice together; arrange in pie crust and set
aside. Combine sugar, salt, flour, butter and one teaspoon cinnamon
together until crumbly; layer over pears. Sprinkle with remaining
cinnamon; bake at 400 degrees for about 40 minutes. Makes
8 servings.

Sugar-Topped Apple Pie

Wanda Scales
Tucson, AZ

A creamy apple pie with a sweet, brown sugar topping…yum!

2 eggs, beaten
1 c. sour cream
1 c. sugar
6 T. all-purpose flour, divided
1 t. vanilla extract
1/4 t. salt

3 c. Red Delicious apples, cored,
    peeled and chopped
9-inch pie crust, unbaked
3 T. butter, softened
1/4 c. brown sugar, packed

Combine eggs and sour cream; blend well. Mix in sugar,
2 tablespoons flour, vanilla and salt; fold in apples. Pour into
pie crust; bake at 375 degrees for 15 minutes. In another bowl,
combine butter, brown sugar and remaining flour together;
sprinkle over pie. Return to oven for 20 to 25 minutes or until
filling is set; cool completely on a wire rack. Makes 8 servings.

A whimsical pie that's terrific for Halloween! After rolling out the top pastry for a two-crust pie, use a small kitchen knife to make a spider web design, being careful not to cut through the pastry. Cut a small hole in the center to vent the steam, place over the filling and bake.

Easy As Pie!

Homemade Apple Pie Filling

Tracy Brookshire
Champaign, IL

You'll be surprised how easy it is to make your own apple pie filling...it's so delicious too!

4-1/2 c. sugar
2 t. cinnamon
3 T. lemon juice
1/4 t. nutmeg
1 t. salt

1 c. cornstarch
10 c. water
7 qts. Jonathan apples, cored,
    peeled and sliced

Mix first 7 ingredients together in a large stockpot; heat until bubbly. Fill sterilized quart canning jars 1/3 full with sauce. Add apples to within 1-1/2 inches of the top. Use a knife to break any bubbles and coat apples with sauce. Wipe rim of jar, place on lid and tighten down ring. Process in a hot water bath for 25 minutes; remove and place on a towel until lid pings and is slightly indented. Makes 8 to 10 quarts.

Add the taste of fresh apple pie to homemade muffins. Just fill the muffin cups halfway with batter, add fruit mixture and top with remaining batter...yum!

Fluffy Lemon-Berry Pie

Elaine Slabinski
Monroe Twp., NJ

One of those desserts that will become a summertime favorite.

1/2 c. cream cheese, softened
1-1/2 c. cold milk
2 3.4-oz. pkgs. instant lemon
   pudding mix
8-oz. container frozen whipped
   topping, thawed and divided

9-inch graham cracker pie crust
Garnish: 1 c. blueberries,
   raspberries or sliced
   strawberries

Blend cream cheese until smooth and creamy; gradually mix in milk. Add pudding mixes; blend 2 minutes or until smooth. Stir in half the whipped topping; spoon into crust. Spread with remaining whipped topping; refrigerate 3 hours or until set. Top with berries before serving. Makes 8 servings.

Send guests home with a delicious reminder of their visit...tiny pies baked in mini muffin tins.

Easy As Pie!

American Pie

Stephanie Collins
Martinsburg, WV

*Red, white & blue...sure to be a hit at the next
Fourth of July picnic!*

21-oz. can blueberry pie filling
10-inch pie crust, baked
8-oz. pkg. cream cheese,
  softened

1 c. powdered sugar
12-oz. container frozen
  whipped topping, thawed
21-oz. can tart cherry pie filling

Pour blueberry pie filling into cooled pie crust; refrigerate
30 minutes. Blend cream cheese and powdered sugar until
smooth; fold in whipped topping. Spread over blueberry pie
filling; refrigerate 30 minutes more. Layer cherry pie filling over
cream cheese mixture; refrigerate at least 4 hours before serving.
Makes 6 servings.

*For an extra-chocolatey chocolate pie, brush the
bottom of a prebaked pie crust with melted
chocolate, let harden and then fill...yum!*

No-Bake Cheesecake

Gail Bellman
Pewaukee, WI

What could be easier?

2 8-oz. pkgs. cream cheese,
   softened
2 c. sour cream
4 t. vanilla extract
2/3 c. sugar

16-oz. container frozen whipped
   topping, thawed
Garnish: 21-oz. can cherry pie
   filling

Blend cream cheese until smooth; add sour cream, vanilla and sugar.
Fold in whipped topping; spread evenly into crust. Refrigerate
overnight. Garnish with pie filling before serving. Makes 12 to
15 servings.

Graham Cracker Crust:

2-1/2 c. graham cracker crumbs   1 c. butter, melted

Toss graham cracker crumbs and butter together; press evenly into a
13"x9" baking dish.

*Coffee adds a rich
taste to chocolate
recipes...just
substitute an
equal amount for
water or milk
in cake, cookie or
brownie recipes.*

Easy As Pie!

Brownie-Ice Cream Pie

Vickie

Whole strawberries dipped into melted chocolate make a beautiful garnish served alongside this tasty pie.

20-oz. pkg. double chocolate
    fudge brownie mix
2 eggs
1/2 c. oil
1/4 c. water

2/3 c. semi-sweet chocolate
    chips
9-inch pie crust, unbaked
Garnish: vanilla ice cream and
    strawberry ice cream topping

Combine brownie mix, eggs, oil and water in a large mixing bowl; stir until blended. Mix in chocolate chips; spoon into crust. Bake at 350 degrees for 40 to 45 minutes; cool completely. Serve pie wedges topped with a scoop of ice cream and strawberry ice cream topping. Makes 8 servings.

Hot Fudge Pie

Hope Davenport
Portland, TX

A soda fountain treat in a pie!

1/2 c. butter, melted
3 T. baking cocoa
1/4 c. all-purpose flour
2 eggs, beaten
1 c. sugar

1 t. vanilla extract
1 c. chopped pecans
9-inch pie crust, unbaked
Garnish: whipped topping and
    hot fudge sauce

Stir butter and cocoa together. Add next 5 ingredients and mix well. Pour into pie crust; bake at 350 degrees for 30 minutes. Cool. Top with garnishes of choice before serving. Makes 8 servings.

Buckeye Pie

Patti Cooper
Delaware, OH

A favorite candy becomes a scrumptious pie!

1/2 c. chocolate chips
1/4 c. corn syrup
1/2 c. creamy peanut butter

1 qt. vanilla ice cream, softened
9-inch chocolate cookie
   crumb crust

Combine chocolate chips, corn syrup and peanut butter in a saucepan; heat over medium heat for 7 to 10 minutes or until melted, stirring constantly. Remove from heat; mix in ice cream, blending until creamy. Pour into pie crust; freeze until firm. Makes 8 servings.

Chocolate Chess Pie

Michele Jones
Houston, TX

I always looked forward to this treat when I visited my grandma.
Passed down from her, it's truly wonderful.

5-oz. can evaporated milk
1-1/2 c. sugar
2 eggs, beaten
1/8 t. salt

3 T. baking cocoa
4 T. butter, melted
1 t. vanilla extract
9-inch pie crust, unbaked

Combine first 7 ingredients together; pour into pie crust. Bake at 350 degrees for 40 to 45 minutes or until set. Makes 8 servings.

Life is uncertain. Eat dessert first.
-Ernestine Ulmer

Easy As Pie!

Pumpkin Pie

Dawn Dobson
Valley City, OH

A classic recipe that's not just for Thanksgiving!

2 c. canned pumpkin
1-1/2 c. evaporated milk
1/2 c. brown sugar, packed
1/2 c. sugar
1/2 t. salt
2 t. pumpkin pie spice

1 t. ground ginger
1/4 t. nutmeg
1/4 t. allspice
1/8 t. ground cloves
2 eggs
9-inch pie crust, unbaked

Combine all of the ingredients except for the pie crust together; mix thoroughly. Pour into pie crust; bake at 425 degrees for 15 minutes. Lower oven temperature to 350 degrees; bake 45 more minutes or until set. Makes 8 servings.

When making double-crust pies, use an assortment of mini cookie cutters to cut shapes out of the top crust. Cut-out pieces can be "glued" around the edge of the crust with beaten egg white...so pretty!

Lemon Meringue Pie

Christi Dickey
Weatherford, TX

I always say this recipe has "fool-proof" meringue...give it a try!

3 eggs, separated
1-1/2 c. sugar
1/3 c. cornstarch
1-1/2 c. water
3 T. butter

4 T. lemon juice
1-1/3 T. lemon zest
9-inch pie crust, baked
1/8 t. salt
1 c. marshmallow creme

In a small mixing bowl, beat egg yolks; set aside. Combine sugar, cornstarch and water in a 2-quart saucepan; bring to a boil over medium heat for one minute, stirring constantly. Remove from heat; gradually blend into beaten egg yolk mixture. Pour back into saucepan; return to boil for one more minute, stirring constantly. Remove from heat; stir in butter, lemon juice and zest. Pour into pie crust; set aside. In a separate mixing bowl, whip egg whites and salt until soft peaks form; gradually blend in marshmallow creme until soft peaks form again. Spread over pie top; completely cover from edge to edge of crust. Bake at 350 degrees for 12 to 15 minutes or until lightly brown. Makes 8 servings.

A knife dipped in water makes cutting a meringue pie simple. There's no need to dry the knife between slices, just wet it again when the meringue begins to stick...so easy!

Easy As Pie!

4-Fruit Pie

Karen Donker
Alliance, NE

Just like the name says, this oh-so-simple pie is filled with four fruits that are terrific when combined.

3/4 c. sugar
1/8 t. ground cloves
1/4 t. allspice
1/4 c. all-purpose flour
1/4 t. nutmeg
1/2 t. cinnamon

1 c. blueberries
1 c. red raspberries
1 c. rhubarb, chopped
1 c. apples, cored, peeled
   and chopped
2 9-inch pie crusts, unbaked

Combine first 6 ingredients; mix well. Gently fold in fruit; toss to coat. Spoon into crust; add top crust and vent. Bake at 400 degrees for 50 to 60 minutes. Makes 8 servings.

Always-Ready Pie Crust Mix

Mary Freireich
Dublin, OH

As a newlywed, I never could make a good pie crust. This recipe, shared with me by my aunt, makes perfect pie crust every time.

6 c. all-purpose flour
2 c. shortening

3 t. salt

Mix ingredients together with a pastry blender until coarse crumbs form; store in an airtight container. When ready to make a pie crust, combine 2 cups mix with cold water, one tablespoon at a time, until dough holds together. Do not add over 6 tablespoons water. Divide dough in half; roll out each half on a lightly floured surface to desired size. Two cups mix makes two, 9-inch pie crusts.

Caramel-Banana Pie

Dorthey Burgess
Mecosta, MI

Sweet, crunchy toffee makes this banana pie special.

14-oz. can sweetened
  condensed milk
2 to 3 bananas, sliced
9-inch graham cracker pie crust
1 c. whipping cream

1/4 c. powdered sugar
2 chocolate-covered toffee
  candy bars, frozen
  and broken

Pour condensed milk into an 8" pie plate; cover with aluminum foil. Pour about 1/4 inch hot water into a 2-quart shallow casserole dish; place covered pie plate in casserole dish. Bake at 425 degrees for one hour and 20 minutes or until milk is thick and caramel colored; add more water when necessary. Carefully remove pan from oven; uncover and set aside. Place bananas on bottom of graham cracker crust; pour caramel mixture over bananas. Cool for at least 30 minutes; while cooling, blend cream and sugar together until fluffy. Spread over caramel layer; sprinkle with toffee bar bits. Chill at least 3 hours or overnight. Makes 8 servings.

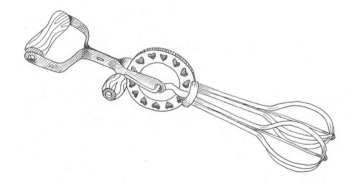

This New Year's Eve, make a resolution that's easy to keep...a list of new desserts to try each month! Friends & family will be happy to help you keep this resolution.

Easy As Pie!

Strawberry Pie

Darci Stavish
Randall, MN

Take the whole family strawberry picking...not only is it fun,
but you'll have this fresh, homemade pie to enjoy too!

1 c. all-purpose flour
2 T. powdered sugar
1/2 c. butter, softened
1-1/2 c. water
3/4 c. sugar
1/8 t. salt

2 T. cornstarch
3-oz. pkg. strawberry
   gelatin mix
4 c. strawberries, hulled
   and sliced
Optional: whipped topping

Combine flour and powdered sugar; cut butter into flour mixture until dough resembles coarse crumbs. Pat into a 9" pie plate; bake at 350 degrees for 15 minutes. Set aside to cool. In a 2-quart saucepan, bring water, sugar, salt and cornstarch to a boil until clear; stir in gelatin until dissolved. Remove from heat; pour 1/4 of the gelatin mixture into pie crust. Fill crust with strawberries; pour remaining gelatin mixture over the top. Chill in refrigerator until set; serve with whipped topping, if desired. Makes 8 to 10 servings.

For a simple dessert, mix sliced strawberries with
strawberry jam or jelly, then fold in whipped
topping. Spoon into a pretty dessert dish
and serve with sugar cookies.

Great Grandma Hall's Shoofly Pie

Kathy Hales
Milford, OH

A gooey, sweet old-fashioned pie. It should really be called molasses pie, but it's whimsically named shoofly because its aroma is so delightful it could lure pesky insects that must be shooed away.

1 c. molasses
1 c. brown sugar, packed
2 c. hot water
1 t. baking soda
2 9-inch pie crusts, unbaked

3 c. all-purpose flour
2 c. sugar
1/2 c. margarine
1 t. baking powder

Mix molasses, brown sugar, water and baking soda together; divide and pour equally into the 2 pie crusts. In another mixing bowl, combine remaining ingredients; sprinkle evenly over molasses mixtures. Bake at 350 degrees for 30 to 45 minutes. Makes 16 servings.

Keep dessert recipes and ideas in a "Happy Endings" journal. They'll always be at your fingertips when you need them!

Easy As Pie!

Sweet Potato Pie

Barb Kietzer
Niles, MI

An easy make-ahead pie...just bake a couple of days ahead and refrigerate. Not only will you save time, but I think it's tastier too.

1/4 c. butter, softened
1/3 c. honey
1/8 t. salt
2 c. sweet potatoes, cooked
   and mashed
3 eggs, beaten
1/2 c. milk

1 t. vanilla extract
1/2 t. cinnamon
1/2 t. nutmeg
1/2 t. ground ginger
8-inch pie crust, unbaked
1 c. pecan halves

Cream butter, honey and salt together; set aside. Combine sweet potatoes, eggs, milk, vanilla and spices; stir into creamed mixture. Pour into pie crust; sprinkle with pecan halves. Bake at 375 degrees for 50 to 55 minutes; cool. Store in refrigerator. Makes 8 servings.

Make a fruit pie even more irresistible...brush peach or apricot syrup on top while the crust is warm, then sprinkle lightly with sugar.

Brown Sugar Puddin' Pies

Angela Nichols
Mt. Airy, NC

Bite-size, brown sugar pies...great for any get-together.

15-ct. pkg. mini phyllo dough
  shells, unbaked
1/2 c. butter, softened
3/4 c. sugar
3/4 c. brown sugar, packed

2 eggs
1/2 c. half-and-half
1/2 t. vanilla extract
Garnish: nutmeg and whipped
  topping

Bake mini shells at 350 degrees for 4 to 5 minutes; set aside. Cream butter and sugars together until light and fluffy; blend in eggs, half-and-half and vanilla. Spoon into pie crusts; sprinkle tops with nutmeg. Bake at 350 degrees for 15 to 20 minutes or until set. Top with a dollop of whipped topping and a dusting of nutmeg before serving. Makes 15 servings.

*Does a pie recipe say to dot the filling with
butter? Just run a vegetable peeler over
a frozen stick of butter...less mess!*

Easy As Pie!

Maple-Pecan Pie

Peggy Bowman
Palisade, CO

*Great anytime, but seems to be just about perfect when
served warm on a chilly autumn day.*

4 eggs, beaten
2/3 c. sugar
1/2 t. salt
6 T. butter, melted

1 c. maple syrup
1-1/2 c. pecan halves
9-inch pie crust, unbaked
Garnish: whipped topping

Blend eggs, sugar, salt, butter and syrup together; set aside. Sprinkle
pecan halves onto pie crust; pour in syrup mixture. Bake at
375 degrees for 15 minutes; lower oven temperature to 350 degrees
and bake 25 more minutes or until center is set. Cool on wire rack.
Serve with whipped topping. Makes 8 servings.

*I just clipped two articles from a current magazine.
One is a diet guaranteed to drop five pounds off my
body in a weekend. The other is a recipe
for a 6-minute pecan pie.*
-Erma Bombeck

Crustless Blackberry Pie

Beth Lang
Bismarck, ND

Bursting with berries!

1-lb. pkg. frozen blackberries
3 T. bread crumbs
3/4 c. plus 2 T. sugar, divided
1 t. cinnamon

2 T. quick-cooking tapioca,
   uncooked
1 c. sour cream
1/4 c. all-purpose flour

Spread blackberries evenly in a 9" pie plate; set aside. In a small bowl, combine bread crumbs, 2 tablespoons sugar and cinnamon; sprinkle half the bread crumb mixture and tapioca over the berries. In another bowl, stir sour cream, remaining sugar and flour together; spread evenly over pie. Sprinkle with remaining bread crumb mixture; bake at 375 degrees for 35 minutes or until bubbly and golden. Makes 8 servings.

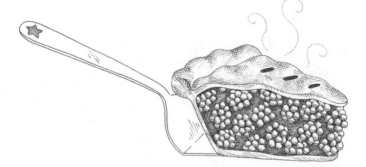

Garnish no-bake pies with thinly sliced oranges or peaches and ice cream pies with crushed candies or chocolate curls for an extra-special finish.

Easy As Pie!

Heartwarming Cherry Pie

Susan Young
Madison, AL

*When this pie is done baking, sometimes I'll open the oven door and
let it sit inside until it's just warm. Not only is it extra warmth
for the kitchen, but the aroma drifts through the entire house!*

3 c. frozen pitted tart red
   cherries, thawed and
   juice reserved
1 c. sugar
1/2 t. salt
1/4 c. all-purpose flour

1 T. butter
4 drops almond extract
4 drops vanilla extract
8 drops red food coloring
2 9-inch pie crusts, unbaked

Pour cherry juice into a 2-quart saucepan; heat over medium heat.
Whisk in sugar, salt and flour; heat until mixture thickens and
becomes glossy. Remove from heat; mix in the cherries, butter,
extracts and food coloring. Pour into bottom pie crust; add top crust,
flute edges and vent top. Bake at 450 degrees for 10 minutes; reduce
oven temperature to 350 and continue baking 40 to 45 minutes.
Makes 8 servings.

*Hosting a cookie exchange? Make invitations
really special with rubber stamps, fabric
snippets and sewing notions.*

Amish Pear Pie

Rosie Bertolini
Santa Rosa, CA

Try this...you'll be surprised and delighted at the combination!

1/3 c. sugar
1 T. cornstarch
1/8 t. salt
5 c. pears, cored, peeled
    and sliced

9-inch pie crust, unbaked
Optional: vanilla ice cream

Mix sugar, cornstarch and salt together; fold in pear slices. Spread in pie crust; sprinkle with topping. Bake on lower oven rack at 425 degrees for 25 to 30 minutes or until pears are tender. Serve with a scoop of ice cream, if desired. Makes 8 servings.

Topping:

1/2 c. all-purpose flour
1/4 t. salt
1/2 c. sugar

1/2 c. shredded sharp
    Cheddar cheese
1/4 c. butter, melted

Combine ingredients together until mixture resembles coarse crumbs.

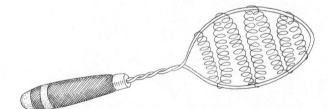

Pears and almonds just seem to go together, so before baking a pear pie, sprinkle finely chopped almonds over the top pie crust...they'll add a terrific flavor and crunch!

Easy As Pie!

Raisin Cream Pie

Kathryn Ingalls
Wellsville, KS

A true family tradition…this pie was made by my Aunt Fran and brought to every family function for over 60 years.

2 c. raisins
water
2 c. whipping cream
2 c. sugar
4 egg yolks, beaten

1 T. butter
6 T. cornstarch
1 t. vanilla extract
8-inch pie crust, baked

Place raisins in a saucepan; cover with water. Heat over medium heat until plump; drain and let cool. Return raisins to saucepan over medium heat; add cream, sugar and egg yolks. Stir in butter until melted. In a small bowl, whisk cornstarch with vanilla and enough water just to make mixture smooth; add to raisin mixture. Cook 5 minutes or until thick; pour into pie crust. Completely cover pie filling with meringue topping; brown meringue under the broiler, about one to 2 minutes. Makes 8 servings.

Meringue

Mary Murray
Gooseberry Patch

Spread meringue so that it touches the inner edge of the whole pie crust…it will keep the meringue from "shrinking."

4 egg whites, room temperature   1/8 t. salt
6 T. sugar

Place egg whites and sugar in a deep mixing bowl; place mixing bowl in a pan of hot water. Stir until egg whites are warmed; add salt. Remove mixing bowl from water; beat egg whites until soft peaks form and appear glossy. Covers an 8-inch pie.

Fresh Peach Pie

Gerri Phillips
Paoli, IN

*There's nothing more delicious than warm, homemade
peach pie topped with a big scoop of ice cream!*

1/3 c. all-purpose flour
1 c. plus 1 T. sugar, divided
1/4 c. butter
10 to 12 peaches, pitted, peeled
   and sliced

2 9-inch pie crusts, unbaked
Optional: ice cream

Combine flour, one cup sugar and butter until crumbly; set aside.
Arrange a layer of peaches on bottom pie crust; sprinkle one
tablespoon of flour mixture on top. Repeat layers until peaches and
flour mixture are gone. Place on the top crust; flute edges and vent.
Sprinkle with remaining sugar; bake at 350 degrees for 45 minutes or
until crust is golden. Serve warm with a scoop of ice cream, if desired.
Makes 8 servings.

*I don't think a really good pie can be made
without a dozen or so children peeking
over your shoulder as you stoop to
look in at it every little while.*
-John Gould

Easy As Pie!

Mom's Rhubarb Pie

Mary Ann Nemecek
Springfield, IL

Growing up, we always had rhubarb in the garden and my Grandpa Pop, who lived with us, took care of it. When Mom was a child, she remembered moving several times, but he always dug up the rhubarb patch and planted it once again at their new home!

1-1/2 c. sugar
3 T. all-purpose flour
1/8 t. salt

2 eggs, beaten
3 c. rhubarb, chopped

Combine sugar, flour and salt; mix well. Add eggs; blend until smooth. Fold in rhubarb; pour into bottom pie crust. Place on top crust; flute edges and vent. Bake at 450 degrees for 10 minutes; reduce oven temperature to 350 degrees, cover pie edges with aluminum foil and bake for an additional 30 minutes. Makes 8 servings.

Crust:

1/2 c. oil
1/4 c. milk

2 c. all-purpose flour
1/8 t. salt

Mix oil and milk together in a medium mixing bowl; set aside. In another mixing bowl, combine flour and salt together; add to milk mixture. Divide dough in half; roll out on a lightly floured surface to a 9-inch circle. Makes two, 9-inch pie crusts.

There are lots of variations to the traditional rhubarb pie, try adding cherries, raisins or strawberries to the recipe for a whole new treat.

Crunchy Peanut Butter Pie

Wendy Lee Paffenroth
Pine Island, NY

A peanut butter-lover's dream!

30 butter cookies, crushed
1/4 c. butter, melted
2 T. water
3/4 c. crunchy peanut butter
8-oz. pkg. cream cheese
1/4 c. butter, softened
1 c. powdered sugar
1 T. almond extract
1 c. frozen whipped topping,
  thawed
Optional: chopped nuts

Combine butter cookies, melted butter and water; press into the bottom a 9" deep-dish pie pan and set aside. Blend peanut butter and cream cheese together until smooth; add butter. Mix in sugar and almond extract; blend well. Fold in whipped topping; spread into pie crust. If desired, sprinkle with chopped nuts; cover with plastic wrap and refrigerate at least 4 hours before serving. Makes 8 servings.

Does a pie recipe call for separating eggs? If so, they're easier to separate when cold, but for the best results, be sure to bring them back to room temperature before using them.

The Icing on the Cake

Overnight Coffee Cake

Cathy Lemoyne
Ontario, Canada

If you decide you just can't wait and want to enjoy this coffee cake right away, go ahead and bake as directed and skip letting it sit overnight…it'll still be moist and delicious.

2 c. all-purpose flour
1 t. baking powder
1 t. baking soda
1/2 t. salt
1 c. sugar
1 c. brown sugar, packed
   and divided

2 t. cinnamon, divided
1 c. buttermilk
2/3 c. butter, melted
2 eggs
1/2 c. chopped pecans, toasted

Combine first 5 ingredients, 1/2 cup brown sugar and one teaspoon cinnamon in a large mixing bowl; add buttermilk, butter and eggs. Blend on low speed until moistened; increase speed to medium and blend 3 additional minutes. Spoon batter into a greased and floured 13"x9" baking pan; set aside. Mix remaining brown sugar, cinnamon and pecans together; sprinkle over batter. Cover; refrigerate overnight. Bake, uncovered, at 350 degrees for 30 minutes or until a toothpick inserted in center removes clean. Makes 12 servings.

Any little girl would love a Barbie cake for her birthday…it's so easy. Just bake a favorite cake recipe in a well-greased, oven-safe bowl. Let the cake cool and invert onto a cake stand. Slip a Barbie into the middle of the cake and pipe on frosting to become her dress…how fun!

The Icing On the Cake

Grandma's Apple-Nut Cake

Danielle Marchand
Tuxedo Park, NY

This recipe originated in Switzerland and was passed down from my great-great grandmother. Every fall, our whole family gathers to go apple picking so we'll have plenty of fresh apples for this cake.

1-1/2 c. sugar
3 eggs
1 c. oil
1-1/2 t. vanilla extract
2 c. all-purpose flour
1 t. baking soda

1/2 t. salt
1 T. cinnamon
2 apples, cored, peeled and
   coarsely chopped
1 c. chopped walnuts or pecans
Garnish: powdered sugar

Mix sugar, eggs, oil and vanilla with a spoon in a large mixing bowl; set aside. In another bowl, combine flour, baking soda, salt and cinnamon; stir into sugar mixture until smooth. Fold in apples and nuts; pour into a greased and floured 13"x9" baking pan. Bake at 375 degrees for 40 minutes; cool. Cut into squares; sprinkle with powdered sugar before serving. Makes 12 to 16 servings.

Make memories with those you love...spend a day baking and sharing favorite recipes.

Toffee-Brown Sugar Cake

Judy Hasenstein
Oconomowoc, WI

*Pecans and toffee combine for a sweet and crunchy filling
in this delicious sour cream cake.*

1 c. margarine
2-1/2 c. sugar, divided
2 eggs
1-1/2 c. sour cream
1 t. vanilla extract
2-1/4 c. all-purpose flour

1 t. baking powder
1 c. chopped pecans
1 c. chocolate-covered toffee
   candy bars, coarsely
   chopped
1 c. brown sugar, packed

Cream margarine and 2 cups sugar together; add eggs, sour cream
and vanilla, blending well. Gradually mix in flour and baking
powder; pour half the batter into a greased and floured Bundt® pan.
In another mixing bowl, combine pecans, candy bars, remaining
sugar and brown sugar together; sprinkle half the mixture over
batter. Repeat layers; bake at 350 degrees for 50 minutes. Cool;
remove from pan. Pour frosting on top before serving. Makes
12 servings.

Frosting:

1-1/2 c. powdered sugar
2 T. butter, softened

1-1/2 t. vanilla extract
1-1/2 T. warm water

Combine until smooth and creamy.

*A gift from the kitchen
is a gift from the heart.
-Unknown*

The Icing On the Cake

Teatime Crumbcake

JoAnn

A delicate treat anytime during the day...this is especially good served with chamomile tea.

2 c. all-purpose flour
1 t. baking powder
1 t. baking soda
1 t. salt
1/2 c. butter, softened
1 c. sugar

1-1/2 t. vanilla extract
3 eggs
1 c. sour cream
1-1/2 c. mini semi-sweet
   chocolate chips

Combine first 4 ingredients together; set aside. In a large mixing bowl, cream butter, sugar and vanilla together; add eggs, one at a time, blending well after each addition. Add in flour mixture alternately with sour cream; fold in chocolate chips. Spread into a greased 13"x9" baking pan; sprinkle with topping. Bake at 350 degrees for 45 to 50 minutes; cool completely. Makes 2 dozen servings.

Topping:

1 T. all-purpose flour
3/4 c. brown sugar, packed
2-1/2 T. butter, softened

3/4 c. chopped nuts
2/3 c. semi-sweet chocolate
   chips

Mix flour, brown sugar and butter together; stir in nuts and chocolate chips, mixing well.

Make a sweet memory and have a tea party for your little girl and her friends! Make it really special: send out pretty invitations, dress up, use real china and treat them to tasty tarts, delicate cakes and herbal tea...they'll love it!

Tutti-Frutti Cake

Michelle Lamp
Slayton, MN

*Just a little taste of chocolate really adds something
special to this cake.*

1 c. sugar
1-1/2 c. all-purpose flour
1 t. baking soda
1/4 t. salt
1 c. less 1 T. milk
2 T. lemon juice
1/2 c. butter, melted

1-oz. sq. baking chocolate,
  melted
1 egg, beaten
1-1/2 c. chopped dates
1/2 c. chopped walnuts
1 t. vanilla extract

Combine first 4 ingredients together; set aside. Stir milk and lemon
juice together; add to flour mixture. Blend in remaining ingredients
in order listed; mix well after each addition. Pour into a greased and
floured 13"x9" baking pan; bake at 350 degrees for 35 to
40 minutes. Makes 12 servings.

Old-Fashioned Yellow Cake

Sue Balfour
Westfield, PA

*Topped with chocolate frosting or whipped cream,
this is a real treat.*

2-1/2 c. all-purpose flour
1-2/3 c. sugar
1 t. salt
2/3 c. shortening

1-1/4 c. milk, divided
3-1/2 t. baking powder
3 eggs
1 t. vanilla extract

Mix flour, sugar, salt, shortening and 3/4 cup milk together; add
baking powder, eggs, vanilla and remaining milk. Pour batter into a
lightly greased and floured 13"x9" baking pan or two, 9" round
baking pans; bake at 350 degrees for 25 to 30 minutes. Cool on a
wire rack. Makes 12 servings.

The Icing On the Cake

Strawberry Cake

Melanie Wallace
Corinth, TX

A fruity sensation!

18-1/2 oz. pkg. white cake mix
3-oz. pkg. strawberry
   gelatin mix
4 eggs

3/4 c. oil
1/2 c. frozen strawberries,
   thawed and undrained
1/2 c. water

Combine ingredients; mix well. Pour into a greased and floured 13"x9" baking pan; bake at 350 degrees for 35 to 40 minutes. Frost before serving. Makes 12 to 15 servings.

Frosting:

1/2 c. frozen strawberries,
   thawed and undrained

4 T. butter, softened
16-oz. pkg. powdered sugar

Blend ingredients together until creamy.

For a guaranteed crumb-free frosting, add a very thin layer of frosting to a cake and refrigerate. When the frosting is firm, go ahead, frost and decorate as desired...it'll be beautiful!

Toffee & Black Walnut Cake

Janet Pastrick
Gooseberry Patch

*Crunchy walnuts and toffee bars are the filling for
this sugar-dusted cake. Served warm from
the oven, it'll disappear quickly!*

2 c. all-purpose flour
1-1/4 c. sugar, divided
1-1/2 t. baking powder
1 t. baking soda
1/2 t. salt
1-1/2 t. vanilla extract
1 c. sour cream
1/2 c. butter, softened

2 eggs
1 c. chopped black walnuts,
　divided
2 t. cinnamon
3 1.4-oz. chocolate-covered
　toffee candy bars, chopped
1/4 c. butter, melted
Garnish: powdered sugar

Combine flour, one cup sugar, baking powder, baking soda, salt,
vanilla, sour cream, softened butter, eggs and 1/2 cup walnuts
together; blend for 3 minutes on low speed. Pour half the batter into
a greased and floured 10" Bundt® pan; set aside. Combine remaining
sugar and cinnamon; sprinkle half over the batter. Repeat layers.
Combine remaining walnuts and toffee bars together; sprinkle over
the top. Drizzle with melted butter; bake at 325 degrees for 45 to
50 minutes. Cool upright for 15 minutes; invert cake and remove
pan. Dust with powdered sugar before serving. Makes
12 to 16 servings.

The Icing On the Cake

Blue-Ribbon Chocolate Cake

Chris Leasure
Radnor, OH

A first-place winner in our county fair's baked goods division!

1/4 c. butter
1/4 c. shortening
2 c. sugar
1 t. vanilla extract
2 eggs

3/4 c. baking cocoa
1-3/4 c. all-purpose flour
1/4 t. baking powder
3/4 t. salt
1-3/4 c. milk

Cream butter, shortening, sugar and vanilla until fluffy; blend in eggs and set aside. Combine cocoa, flour, baking powder and salt together; add alternately with milk to sugar mixture. Blend well; pour into 2 round, greased and floured 9" baking pans. Bake at 350 degrees for 30 to 35 minutes; cool and frost. Makes 16 servings.

Frosting:

6 T. butter, softened
1/2 c. baking cocoa
2-2/3 c. powdered sugar

1/3 c. milk
1 t. vanilla extract

Cream butter; add cocoa and powdered sugar alternately with milk. Mix in vanilla; blend until smooth and creamy.

Spread joy to a neighbor...deliver a homemade treat, warm from the oven.

Nutty Raisin Cake

Roxanne Bixby
West Franklin, NH

Spread slices with softened cream cheese...so good.

1 c. less 1 T. milk
2 T. lemon juice
1 c. brown sugar, packed
1/2 c. oil
1 t. baking soda
1 t. nutmeg

3/4 c. raisins
2 c. all-purpose flour
1 t. cinnamon
1/2 t. ground cloves
1/2 c. chopped nuts

Stir milk and lemon juice together in a large mixing bowl; blend in remaining ingredients. Pour into a greased 9"x5" loaf pan; bake at 350 degrees for one hour or until a toothpick inserted into the center removes clean. Makes 8 servings.

Mom will love a spring bonnet cake! Use a round, oven-proof bowl to bake the batter in, cool and invert cake on a cake stand. Line sugar cookies around the edge for the brim, and then frost and decorate.

The Icing On the Cake

Brown Sugar-Oatmeal Cake

Lori Bryan
Huntsville, AR

Always better if made a day in advance.

1-1/4 c. boiling water
1 c. long-cooking oats,
    uncooked
2 eggs, beaten
1 c. sugar
1 c. brown sugar, packed

1/2 c. oil
1-1/2 c. all-purpose flour
1 t. baking soda
1 t. salt
1 t. cinnamon

Pour boiling water over oats in a small mixing bowl; set aside. Mix eggs, sugars and oil together; add remaining ingredients. Blend in oatmeal mixture; pour into a greased 13"x9" baking pan. Bake at 350 degrees for 30 to 35 minutes. Spread topping over warm cake; broil until topping is golden and crunchy, about 2 minutes. Makes 20 servings.

Topping:

1 c. flaked coconut
1 c. brown sugar, packed
6 T. butter, melted

1/2 c. chopped pecans
1/4 c. evaporated milk

Mix ingredients together.

For an even richer-tasting chocolate cake, use dark brown sugar in the recipe!

Mystery Mocha Cake

Cathy Price
Scottsdale, AZ

Just how those ingredients added on top of the batter magically end up as a rich gooey sauce on the bottom...that's the mystery!

1-1/4 c. sugar, divided
1 c. all-purpose flour
2 t. baking powder
1/8 t. salt
1-oz. sq. unsweetened baking
   chocolate

2 T. butter
1/2 c. milk
1 t. vanilla extract
1/2 c. brown sugar, packed
4 T. baking cocoa
1 c. coffee, cold

Combine 3/4 cup sugar, flour, baking powder and salt together; set aside. Melt chocolate with butter in a double boiler; add to flour mixture. In another bowl, mix milk and vanilla together; add to flour mixture, stirring well. Pour batter into a greased 9"x9" baking pan; set aside. Combine brown sugar, remaining sugar and cocoa together; sprinkle over batter. Pour coffee on top; do not mix. Bake at 350 degrees for 40 minutes. Makes 12 to 16 servings.

Chocolate "leaves" make a yummy cake garnish. Start with edible leaves, rinse clean and pat dry. Place the leaves on wax paper and brush with melted chocolate. When completely cool, gently peel off the leaf and discard...arrange the chocolate leaves on a frosted cake or cupcake.

The Icing On the Cake

Banana Cake

Heidi Harpestad
Eston, Saskatchewan

Moist and sweet with a creamy whipped frosting.

2-1/4 c. all-purpose flour
1-2/3 c. sugar
1-1/4 t. baking powder
1-1/4 t. baking soda
1 t. salt

1 c. oil
4 eggs, beaten
2/3 c. milk
1 T. vinegar
1-1/4 c. bananas, mashed

Combine first 7 ingredients together; set aside. In a small bowl, mix milk with vinegar; add to flour mixture. Fold in bananas; stir well. Pour batter into 2 round, greased and floured, 9" baking pans; bake at 350 degrees for 45 to 50 minutes. Cool on a wire rack; frost. Makes 8 to 10 servings.

Frosting:

3-1/2 oz. pkg. instant banana
   pudding mix

2 c. frozen whipped topping,
   thawed

Blend together until well mixed.

Strawberry Cream Tunnel Cake

*Susie Garrett
Grand Prairie, TX*

Angel food cake with a sweet, creamy filling.

1 prepared angel food cake
8-oz. pkg. cream cheese,
  softened
14-oz. can sweetened
  condensed milk

1/3 c. lemon juice
3/4 t. almond extract
2 c. strawberries, sliced
16-oz. container frozen
  whipped topping, thawed

Cut a one-inch thick crosswise slice from the top of the cake; set aside. Create a tunnel in the cake by cutting around the inside of the cake one inch from center and one inch from outer edge of cake. Remove cake from center, leaving a one-inch thick cake bottom, walls and center; set aside. Blend cream cheese until fluffy; add milk, blending until smooth. Stir in lemon juice and almond extract; mix well. Fold in removed cubes of cake and strawberries; spoon into cake tunnel. Replace top slice of cake; frost with whipped topping and refrigerate until set. Makes 12 to 18 servings.

Cheer on your favorite team! Bake a cake in a 13"x9" baking dish and cool. Cut cake diagonally to form a pair of pennants, and then frost in school colors.

The Icing On the Cake

Angel Food Cake

Lori Burris
Gooseberry Patch

When time allows, make this heavenly cake from scratch...it's so much simpler than you think.

10 egg whites
1/2 t. salt
1-1/2 t. cream of tartar

1-1/2 t. vanilla extract
1-1/4 c. cake flour
1-3/4 c. sugar

Beat egg whites and salt in a large bowl at high speed of an until foamy; add cream of tartar and vanilla, beating until soft peaks form. In another bowl, mix flour and sugar together; add to egg white mixture, beating well. Fold into an ungreased 10" tube pan; draw knife through batter to remove air bubbles. Bake at 375 degrees for 30 to 40 minutes or until top springs back when pressed. Invert pan, placing center over top of a bottle; cool one hour then remove cake from pan. Makes 12 to 16 servings.

If a recipe calls for a tube pan and there's not one handy, make your own. Set a clean, empty can in the middle of a deep cake pan. Fill the can with beans to keep it in place, then carefully pour the batter around the can...so simple!

Apple Blossom Cake

Jo Ann Barger
Urbana, OH

A family favorite, especially during harvest time.

1-1/4 c. oil
2 c. sugar
2 eggs
1 t. vanilla extract
1 c. chopped nuts
3 c. apples, cored, peeled
   and chopped

3 c. all-purpose flour
1-1/2 t. baking soda
1/2 t. salt
1 t. cinnamon
1 t. nutmeg
Garnish: whipped topping

Blend oil, sugar and eggs together; add vanilla, nuts and apples. In another mixing bowl, combine remaining ingredients; stir into apple mixture. Pour into a greased 13"x9" baking pan; sprinkle with topping. Bake at 350 degrees 35 to 50 minutes, or until a toothpick inserted in the center removes clean; cool. Serve with a dollop of whipped topping. Makes 24 servings.

Topping:

1/3 c. sugar
1 t. cinnamon

1/2 c. chopped nuts

Toss ingredients together until nuts are well coated.

Celebrate Friendship Day, the first Sunday in August, with a dessert party. Sweet treats, along with plenty of time to chat, will make for a fun-filled afternoon!

The Icing On the Cake

Rich Spice Cake

Naomi Cycak
Ligonier, PA

A family favorite from one of my Grandmother's oldest cookbooks dated 1928.

2 c. plus 1 T. all-purpose flour.
   divided
2 t. cinnamon
1 t. ground cloves
1 t. allspice
1/2 t. nutmeg
1 t. baking soda

1 c. less 2 T. milk
2 T. vinegar
1/2 c. shortening
2 c. brown sugar, packed
3 egg yolks, beaten
2 egg whites, stiffly beaten
1 c. raisins

Sift 2 cups flour, cinnamon, cloves, allspice, nutmeg and baking soda together; set aside. Stir milk and vinegar together; set aside. Cream shortening and sugar together in a large mixing bowl; add egg yolks. Gradually mix in flour mixture alternately with milk; fold in egg whites. Toss raisins with remaining flour; fold into batter. Pour into two, 8" round baking pans; bake at 350 degrees for 30 minutes or until toothpick inserted into center removes clean. Cool; frost with caramel icing. Makes 8 to 12 servings.

Caramel Icing:

2 c. brown sugar, packed
1 c. whipping cream

1 T. butter
1 t. vanilla extract

Heat the sugar and cream together in a heavy saucepan until soft ball stage, or 234 to 240 degrees on a candy thermometer. Stir in butter and vanilla; remove from heat. Blend until desired spreading consistency is reached.

Ginger Ale Pound Cake

Carol Hickman
Kingsport, TN

This lemony pound cake has a "secret" ingredient to keep it moist and delicious…ginger ale!

2-1/3 c. sugar
1 c. butter, softened
1/3 c. shortening
5 eggs

2 t. lemon flavoring
3 c. self-rising flour
3/4 c. ginger ale

Cream sugar, butter and shortening together; add eggs, one at a time, blending well after each addition. Mix in lemon flavoring; add flour and ginger ale. Pour batter into a greased Bundt® pan; bake at 325 degrees for one hour and 15 minutes. Cool in pan 20 to 30 minutes; remove cake and cool completely. Makes 10 to 12 servings.

Strawberry Shortcake

T.R. Ralston
Gooseberry Patch

Very, very simple and looks so pretty.

2 c. all-purpose flour
3 t. baking powder
1/2 t. salt
1/2 c. sugar

1/3 c. butter, melted
1 c. milk
Garnish: half-and-half, sliced
and whole strawberries

Combine dry ingredients together; mix in butter and milk. Stir; spread into a greased 13"x9" baking pan. Bake at 450 degrees for 12 to 15 minutes; cool. Cut into squares; slice horizontally. Spoon strawberries on bottom slice; pour one tablespoon of half-and-half over the strawberries. Top with remaining slice; garnish with a whole strawberry. Makes 12 to 15 servings.

The Icing On the Cake

Mini Blueberry-Coconut Pound Cakes

Kathy Theis
Ojai, CA

Topped with golden, toasted coconut, these bite-size blueberry cakes make a terrific after-school treat.

1/4 c. butter, softened
3/4 c. sugar
2 t. lime zest
2 eggs
5 T. whipping cream

1 c. all-purpose flour
1/4 t. salt
1/2 c. plus 3 T. flaked coconut, divided
1/2 c. blueberries

Cream butter, sugar and zest until light and fluffy; add eggs, one at a time, beating well after each addition. Blend in cream, flour and salt on low speed until just combined; stir in 1/2 cup coconut and blueberries. Spoon batter into greased and floured muffin cups until 1/2 full; smooth tops. Sprinkle with remaining coconut; bake at 350 degrees for 25 minutes or until edges are golden. Invert onto a wire rack to cool. Makes about 9 servings.

Day will break and you'll awake
and start to bake a sugar cake.
-Irving Caesar

Peanut Butter Sheet Cake

Michelle Beal
Parkersburg, WV

An easy-to-make recipe of my father's that's so good.

1/2 c. creamy peanut butter
1/2 c. butter
1/2 c. applesauce
1 c. water
2 c. sugar

2 c. all-purpose flour
2 eggs
1/2 c. milk
1 t. baking soda
1 t. vanilla extract

Combine first 4 ingredients in a saucepan; bring to a boil. Remove from heat; mix in remaining ingredients. Pour into a lightly greased jelly roll pan; bake at 350 degrees for 20 to 25 minutes. Cool; frost with peanut butter icing. Makes 24 to 30 servings.

Peanut Butter Icing:

1/2 c. creamy peanut butter
1/2 c. butter
1/3 c. milk

1-lb. pkg. powdered sugar
1 t. vanilla extract

Place first 3 ingredients in a saucepan; bring to a boil. Remove from heat; blend in powdered sugar and vanilla until smooth and creamy.

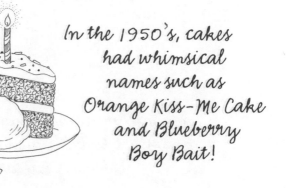

In the 1950's, cakes had whimsical names such as Orange Kiss-Me Cake and Blueberry Boy Bait!

The Icing On the Cake

Moon Cake

Cheryl Wiedrich
Beulah, ND

A cake that tastes out of this world!

1/2 c. butter, softened
1 c. water
1 c. all-purpose flour
4 eggs
2 3-1/2 oz. pkgs. instant white
　　chocolate pudding mix,
　　prepared

8-oz. container frozen whipped
　　topping, thawed
Garnish: butterscotch syrup

Bring butter and water to a boil; stir in flour until a ball forms. Remove from heat; add eggs, one at a time, mixing thoroughly after each addition. Spread into a greased 15"x10" baking pan; bake at 400 degrees for 30 minutes or until golden. Cool; spread with prepared pudding. Frost with whipped topping; drizzle with butterscotch syrup. Refrigerate until firm. Makes 24 to 30 servings.

Popcorn Cake

Debra Waggoner
Grand Island, NE

Children of all ages love to make and eat this cake!

1-1/4 c. margarine
16-oz. pkg. marshmallows
20 c. popped popcorn

1 c. candy-coated chocolate
　　mini baking bits
1/2 c. peanuts

Melt margarine and marshmallows in a double boiler; pour over popcorn, mixing well. Stir in remaining ingredients; press into a buttered angel food cake pan. Cool; invert cake and remove pan. Makes 12 to 16 servings.

Northeastern Blueberry Cake

Wendy Lee Paffenroth
Pine Island, NY

*If you're lucky enough to live where blueberries grow wild,
spend an afternoon berry picking. Tossed in this
scrumptious cake, they're worth the effort!*

1/4 c. butter	1/2 t. nutmeg
1 c. sugar	1/2 t. lemon zest
1 egg	1 c. milk
2-1/2 c. all-purpose flour	3 c. blueberries
1 t. baking powder	

Cream butter and sugar together; add egg, blending well. In another
mixing bowl, combine flour, baking powder, nutmeg and lemon zest.
Add alternately to creamed mixture with milk; fold in blueberries.
Pour batter into a greased and floured 10" Bundt® pan; bake at
350 degrees for 45 to 50 minutes or until a toothpick inserted
into center removes clean. Cool completely; frost. Makes 12 to
15 servings.

Frosting:

8-oz. pkg. cream cheese, softened	1/8 t. lemon zest
1/2 c. powdered sugar	1 T. milk
	1/2 t. vanilla extract

Blend cream cheese until light and fluffy; add remaining ingredients.
Mix until smooth and creamy.

*Before adding to cake batter,
toss nuts, raisins, dried or
fresh fruit in flour...it keeps
them from sinking to the
bottom of the cake!*

The Icing On the Cake

Mexican Fruit Cake

Lynne Hunker
Fostoria, OH

A light and fruity dessert our family always looks forward to enjoying.

2 c. all-purpose flour
2 c. sugar
2 eggs
2 t. baking soda

2-1/2 c. crushed pineapple, undrained
1 c. chopped walnuts

Combine ingredients together; pour into a greased and floured 13"x9" baking pan. Bake at 350 degrees for 35 to 45 minutes; spread with topping while cake is still warm. Makes 15 servings.

Topping:

3-oz. pkg. cream cheese, softened
1 t. vanilla extract

1 c. powdered sugar
1/4 c. margarine

Blend all ingredients until smooth and creamy.

Don't tuck Grandma's beautiful cake plates away, saving them for "someday." Get them out and enjoy them now! Each time they're used, they'll be a sweet reminder of her homemade treats.

Hickory Nut Cake

Vickie

*Can't find hickory nuts? Substitute pecans or walnuts
in this recipe for an equally nutty taste.*

2 c. sugar
2/3 c. butter, softened
3 eggs
2 t. baking powder
1/4 t. salt

2-1/2 c. all-purpose flour
1 c. milk
1-1/2 t. vanilla extract
1 c. chopped pecans

Cream sugar and butter together; add eggs. Blend on medium speed
for 2 minutes; set aside. Mix dry ingredients together in a separate
mixing bowl; add to sugar mixture alternately with milk. Stir in
vanilla and nuts; pour into a greased and floured 13"x9" baking pan.
Bake at 325 degrees for 45 to 50 minutes; cool and frost. Makes
12 to 15 servings.

Frosting:

1/2 c. butter, melted
1 c. brown sugar, packed
1/3 c. milk
2-1/4 c. powdered sugar

1 t. vanilla extract
Optional: 1/2 c. chopped
    hickory nuts

Bring butter and brown sugar to a boil in a 2-quart saucepan; boil for
2 minutes. Slowly add milk; return to a boil. Remove from heat; cool
to lukewarm. Blend in powdered sugar and vanilla until smooth; stir
in nuts, if desired.

*For quick release, line cake bottoms with
parchment paper that's been lightly coated
with oil and dusted with flour, or try dusting
with baking cocoa for chocolate cakes.*

The Icing On the Cake

Chocolate Chip Cake

Emily Buchanan
Grand Junction, CO

*Even though my family says they don't like dates, they all love it
when I make this easy no-frost cake!*

1 c. chopped dates	2 eggs
1 c. boiling water	1-3/4 c. all-purpose flour
1 t. baking soda	2 t. baking cocoa
1 c. margarine	1 c. chocolate chips
1 c. sugar	1 c. chopped nuts

Add dates to boiling water; stir in baking soda and set aside. Cream
margarine, sugar and eggs together; add flour and cocoa, mixing
well. Blend in date mixture; pour into a 13"x9" baking pan. Sprinkle
with chocolate chips and nuts; press slightly into batter. Bake at
350 degrees for 35 to 40 minutes. Makes 12 to 15 servings.

*Strawberry "flowers" are a sweet garnish on a
chocolate-frosted cake. Slice each strawberry in
quarters, being careful not to cut through the stem,
and then gently press a cranberry in the center
to create a "flower".*

Hot Fudge Cake

Joanna Whelan
Mayfield, KY

Served warm and topped with a scoop of vanilla ice cream,
this won't last long...better make two!

1 c. all-purpose flour
3/4 c. sugar
6 T. baking cocoa, divided
2 t. baking powder
1/4 t. salt
1/2 c. milk

2 T. oil
1 t. vanilla extract
1 c. brown sugar, packed
1-3/4 c. hot water
Optional: whipped topping or
　　ice cream

Combine flour, sugar, 2 tablespoons cocoa, baking powder and salt
together; mix in milk, oil and vanilla until smooth. Spread in an
ungreased 9"x9" baking pan. In a separate bowl, mix remaining
cocoa and brown sugar together; sprinkle over batter. Pour hot water
over the top; do not stir. Bake at 350 degrees for 35 to 40 minutes;
serve warm with a scoop of whipped topping or ice cream, if desired.
Makes 12 to 16 servings.

An old-fashioned cake or pie auction
makes a great fundraiser. Tuck each treat in a
decorated box and let the bidding begin!

The Icing On the Cake

Spicy Gingerbread Cake

Shelly Richards
Wenatchee, WA

Prep time is so short, you can whip this up in no time.

1 c. sugar
2/3 c. oil
1/2 t. salt
1 c. molasses
1 t. baking soda
1 c. hot water or coffee

2-1/2 c. all-purpose flour
1 t. cinnamon
1/2 t. ground cloves
1/2 t. ground ginger
2 eggs

Combine ingredients together in order listed; pour into a lightly greased 13"x9" baking pan. Bake at 350 degrees for 35 minutes. Makes 24 servings.

Put a sparkler on top of a favorite cake for a dessert not soon forgotten!

Fudge Cake

Stella Hickman
Gooseberry Patch

*With joy, I recently found this childhood favorite
handed down from my grandmother.*

2 c. all-purpose flour
2 t. baking powder
1/2 t. cinnamon
1/2 t. nutmeg
1-3/4 c. sugar
1/2 c. milk

3/4 c. butter
2 eggs
1 c. mashed potatoes, warm
2 1-oz. sqs. unsweetened
    baking chocolate, melted
1 c. chopped pecans

Combine dry ingredients; set aside. Blend butter and eggs together;
add milk. Mix in dry ingredients; add mashed potatoes and
chocolate. Fold in pecans; mix well. Pour equally into two,
8"x8" greased and floured baking pans; bake at 375 degrees for
35 to 40 minutes. Cool completely; frost with caramel frosting.
Makes 12 servings.

Caramel Frosting:

1 c. brown sugar, packed
1/4 c. milk
2 T. shortening
2 T. butter

1 t. vanilla extract
1-1/2 c. powdered sugar
milk

Bring first 4 ingredients to a boil; remove from heat and let cool.
Add vanilla, powdered sugar and enough milk to reach desired
consistency, blending until smooth.

*Here's a handy tip: before adding shortening to a
recipe, run the measuring cups under water...the
shortening will slip right out!*

The Icing On the Cake

Pumpkin Roll

Linda Guth
Metamora, IL

Pumpkin rolls are so beautiful and you'd be surprised how simple they are to make. Everyone will be impressed!

3 eggs
1 c. sugar
2/3 c. canned pumpkin
1 t. lemon juice
1 c. all-purpose flour
2 t. cinnamon

1 t. ground ginger
1 t. baking powder
1-1/2 t. salt
3/4 c. chopped walnuts
1/2 c. powdered sugar

Beat eggs on high speed for 5 minutes; blend in sugar, pumpkin and lemon juice. In a separate bowl, combine next 5 ingredients; add to pumpkin mixture. Pour into a well-greased and floured jelly roll pan; top with walnuts. Bake at 325 degrees for 15 minutes; loosen edges and invert onto a dishtowel sprinkled with powdered sugar. Roll towel and cake up jelly roll-style; cool. Unroll cake; spread with filling. Re-roll cake with filling this time but not with towel; refrigerate until firm. Slice to serve. Makes 2 dozen servings.

Filling:

8-oz. pkg. cream cheese,
   softened

1 c. powdered sugar
2 T. butter, softened

Blend until smooth and creamy.

For every cup of sugar, stir in 2 tablespoons of orange or lemon zest. Added to cake recipes, it adds a yummy citrus taste!

Banana Split Cake

Karen Herring
Slaughter, LA

Drizzle with hot fudge sauce for a real treat!

1 c. butter, melted
2-1/2 c. graham cracker crumbs
2 8-oz. pkgs. cream cheese,
    softened
1-1/2 c. sugar
4 bananas, sliced
2 20-oz. cans crushed
    pineapple, drained

16-oz. container frozen
    whipped topping, thawed
2 c. chopped pecans
16-oz. jar maraschino cherries,
    drained

Mix butter and graham crackers together; press into the bottom of a 13"x9" baking pan. In a mixing bowl, blend cream cheese and sugar together; spread over graham cracker crust. Layer banana slices on the cream cheese; pour crushed pineapple over the top. Spread whipped topping over the pineapple layer; sprinkle pecans evenly on top. Decorate with cherries; refrigerate until firm. Makes 15 to 18 servings.

An old-fashioned cake walk is still fun today! Played like musical chairs, each person stands in front of a number placed on the floor. When the music stops, a number is called out and whoever is standing nearest that number gets to take their pick of the baked goodies.

The Icing On the Cake

Carrot Cake

Shari Miller
Hobart, IN

Making this cake always brings back fond memories of my dear friend Dona. She shared this recipe with me 20 years ago and it's continued to be a favorite.

2 c. all-purpose flour
1-1/2 t. baking soda
2 t. baking powder
2 t. cinnamon
1-1/2 c. oil

2 c. sugar
4 eggs
2 c. carrots, grated
15-1/4 oz. can crushed
    pineapple, drained

Combine ingredients together; blend well. Pour into a 13"x9" greased and floured baking pan; bake at 350 degrees for 35 to 40 minutes. Cool; frost with cream cheese frosting while still warm. Makes 12 to 15 servings.

Cream Cheese Frosting:

1/2 c. margarine, softened
8-oz. pkg. cream cheese,
    softened

1 t. vanilla extract
1-lb. pkg. powdered sugar

Blend ingredients together until smooth and creamy.

LUSCIOUS LEMON

Heavenly Angel Food

Strawberry Supreme

CAKE WALK

Chocolate-Zucchini Cake

Mary Patenaude
Norwich, CT

Why make just zucchini bread with all that summertime bounty?

2 c. sugar
1 c. oil
3 eggs
2-1/2 c. all-purpose flour
1/4 c. baking cocoa
1 t. baking soda

1/4 t. baking powder
1/4 t. salt
1/2 c. milk
1 T. vanilla extract
2 c. zucchini, shredded

Combine sugar and oil; add eggs, one at a time, blending after each addition. In a separate mixing bowl, combine dry ingredients; gradually add to egg mixture alternately with milk. Stir in vanilla and zucchini; pour into a greased 15"x10" baking pan. Bake at 375 degrees for 25 minutes; remove cake to wire rack. Frost while still hot. Makes 20 servings.

Frosting:

1/2 c. butter
1/4 c. baking cocoa
6 T. evaporated milk

4 c. powdered sugar
1 T. vanilla extract

Blend all ingredients together until smooth and creamy.

Cut cake into cubes and layer in dessert dishes with pudding, gelatin or fruit...a tasty dessert just like Mom used to make.

The Icing On the Cake

Double Trouble

Jennifer Licon-Conner
Gooseberry Patch

This doubles as my birthday cake when a scoop of chocolate ice cream and hot fudge sauce are added!

1-3/4 c. all-purpose flour
1-1/2 t. baking soda
1/2 t. salt
1/2 c. butter, softened
2/3 c. sugar
3/4 c. brown sugar, packed
2 eggs

1-1/2 t. vanilla extract
1/2 c. sour cream
4 1-oz. sqs. unsweetened baking chocolate, melted and cooled
1 c. buttermilk

Combine flour, baking soda and salt; set aside. In a large bowl, cream butter until light and fluffy; add sugars and mix one minute. Add eggs, one at a time, blending well after each addition; mix in vanilla. Blend in sour cream; mix for 30 seconds. Stir in melted chocolate; mix well. Add flour mixture to chocolate mixture alternately with buttermilk; pour batter into 2 round, greased and floured, 8" baking pans. Bake at 350 degrees for 25 to 35 minutes; cool. Frost top of one cake; place second cake on top. Frost top and sides of cake. Makes 8 servings.

Frosting:

3 1-oz. sqs. unsweetened baking chocolate
14-oz. can sweetened condensed milk

1/2 c. butter, softened
2 t. vanilla extract

Heat chocolate, milk and butter over low heat; stir constantly until melted and thickened, about 3 minutes. Remove from heat; add vanilla. Let cool 5 minutes before frosting cake.

English Tea Cake

Kathy Boyd
Port Murray, NJ

*Why not enjoy the English tradition of afternoon tea? Take time
to sit back, relax and enjoy this with a cup of hot tea.*

1 c. sugar
1 c. butter, melted
2 eggs
2 c. all-purpose flour
1/2 t. baking powder

1/8 t. salt
6-oz. jar maraschino cherries,
    undrained
1 c. raisins

Combine sugar with butter in a small saucepan over low heat until
dissolved; remove from heat. Blend in eggs; add flour, baking
powder and salt, mixing well. Fold in cherries and raisins; stir gently.
Pour into a greased and floured 9"x5" loaf pan; bake at 275 degrees
for 2 hours. Makes 8 servings.

*Dainty petits-fours can be made in no time.
Just cut one-inch squares from a single layer
cake and top each with a chocolatey glaze
or rich royal icing...yummy!*

The Icing On the Cake

Raspberry & Chocolate Tea Cakes

Pat Habiger
Spearville, KS

Surprise Mom on Mother's Day with these delicious little cakes.

1-1/2 c. all-purpose flour	1/2 c. butter, melted
1/4 c. sugar	1/2 c. milk
1/4 c. brown sugar, packed	1 egg
2 t. baking powder	2 c. mini chocolate chips
1/4 t. salt	1/3 c. seedless raspberry jam

In a large bowl, stir flour, sugars, baking powder and salt together;
set aside. In another mixing bowl, combine butter, milk and egg; add
to flour mixture, stirring until just combined. Fold in chocolate
chips; fill 12 paper-lined muffin cups half full with batter. Spoon
one teaspoon raspberry jam into each center; top with remaining
batter until 2/3 full. Bake at 350 degrees for 20 to 25 minutes.
Makes 14 to 16.

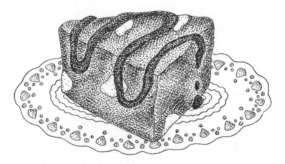

On days when warmth is the most important
need of the human heart, the kitchen
is the place you can find it.
-E.B. White

Red Velvet Cake

Marion Pfeifer
Smyrna, DE

I've found that the men in our family just love this cake! It's always requested for birthdays, graduations or any special gathering.

1/2 c. shortening
2 eggs
1-1/2 c. sugar
1 t. vanilla extract
1-1/2 T. red food coloring
2 c. all-purpose flour

1 t. baking soda
3/4 t. salt
3 T. baking cocoa
1 c. buttermilk
1 T. vinegar

Cream shortening, eggs, sugar, vanilla and food coloring together in a large mixing bowl; set aside. Combine flour, baking soda, salt and cocoa together; set aside. Mix buttermilk and vinegar together; add to sugar mixture alternately with flour mixture. Pour batter into 2 round, greased and floured, 9" baking pans; bake at 350 degrees for 30 to 35 minutes. Cool; frost with icing. Makes 8 to 10 servings.

Best-Ever Soft Icing:

3 T. all-purpose flour
3/4 c. milk
3/4 c. butter, softened

3/4 t. vanilla extract
3/4 c. sugar

Stir flour and milk together in a saucepan over low heat until thick; pour into a mixing bowl. Allow mixture to cool; blend in remaining ingredients until fluffy, about 10 minutes.

Dress up a one-layer cake in minutes by turning it into a layered torte. Slice the cake horizontally and layer on prepared pudding. Replace the top half of the cake and frost...oh-so simple!

The Icing On the Cake

Ice Cream Cone Cakes

Kris Lammers
Gooseberry Patch

Cones that don't melt...my family loves 'em!

2/3 c. all-purpose flour
1/3 c. baking cocoa
1 t. baking powder
1/8 t. salt
2 T. margarine, softened

1/2 c. sugar
1 egg white
1/2 t. vanilla extract
2/3 c. buttermilk
6 flat-bottomed ice cream cones

Combine dry ingredients together in a small bowl; set aside. Cream margarine and sugar in a large mixing bowl; add egg white and vanilla, blending well. Alternately mix in flour mixture and buttermilk; stir until smooth. Fill cones to within 1/2 inch of the top; carefully set on an ungreased baking sheet. Bake at 375 degrees for 35 minutes; cool on wire racks. Frost. Makes 6.

Frosting:

3/4 c. powdered sugar
1 T. margarine, softened

1 t. buttermilk
3/4 t. vanilla extract

Blend ingredients together until smooth and creamy.

Pear Preserves Cake

Kathleen Jarrett
Fredericksburg, VA

For a beautiful finishing touch, lay a pretty stencil on top of the cooled cake, dust with powdered sugar and then gently remove the stencil...so lovely!

1 c. shortening
2-1/2 c. sugar
4 eggs
1 T. vanilla extract
3-1/4 c. all-purpose flour
3/4 t. baking soda
1 t. cinnamon

1 t. ground cloves
1 t. allspice
1 c. buttermilk
11-1/2 oz. jar pear preserves
1 c. chopped pecans
Optional: powdered sugar

Combine ingredients in order listed; pour into a greased and floured, 10" Bundt® pan. Bake at 325 degrees for one hour and 20 minutes; cool in pan 10 minutes. Remove from pan; cool completely. Dust with powdered sugar, if desired. Makes 12 to 15 servings.

Make a triple-layer cake extra tasty. Sprinkle chocolate chips, crushed candies, nuts, mini baking bits or toasted coconut on each layer after it's frosted...yum!

Chocolate... striking it rich

Chocolate Supreme

Glenda Hubbs
Maryville, TN

It's a tradition to let our children take turns choosing dessert for special holidays...here is my son's favorite!

1/2 c. butter, melted
1 c. self-rising flour
1/3 c. brown sugar, packed
1/2 c. chopped pecans
8-oz. pkg. cream cheese, softened
1 c. powdered sugar

16-oz. container frozen whipped topping, thawed and divided
2 3-1/2 oz. pkgs. instant chocolate pudding mix
3 c. milk
Optional: chopped pecans

Coat bottom of a 13"x9" baking dish with butter; set aside. Combine flour, brown sugar and pecans together; press into bottom of baking dish. Bake at 300 degrees for 15 minutes; cool. In a medium mixing bowl, blend cream cheese, powdered sugar and one cup whipped topping together; spread over crust. In another bowl, mix pudding with milk; spread evenly over cream cheese layer. Top with layer of remaining whipped topping; sprinkle with additional chopped pecans, if desired. Chill 3 to 4 hours before serving. Makes 18 servings.

Having a mug of chocolatey cocoa? Make it irresistible by adding a favorite hard candy and stir until melted. Try orange, peppermint or raspberry...great for coffee too!

Chocolate... Striking It Rich

Chocolate Chip Scones

Ann Brouillette
Sioux City, IA

Try adding raspberry chips for a rich chocolate-raspberry taste.

2 c. all-purpose flour
2 T. sugar
2 t. baking powder
1/2 t. baking soda
1/4 t. salt

1/2 c. chilled butter
1/2 c. mini semi-sweet
   chocolate chips
1 egg, beaten
1/2 c. milk

Combine flour, sugar, baking powder, baking soda and salt; cut in butter until mixture resembles coarse crumbs. Toss in chocolate chips. Mix in egg and milk; stir until just moistened. Form dough into a ball; knead for 10 strokes. Pat into an 8-inch circle; cut into 6 wedges. Space each wedge about one inch apart on a greased baking sheet; bake at 375 degrees for 15 to 18 minutes. Remove to wire rack to cool; drizzle with icing. Makes 6 servings.

Icing:

1 c. powdered sugar
1/4 t. vanilla extract

1 T. milk

Whisk together until smooth and creamy.

Nuts just take up space where chocolate ought to be.
-Unknown

Chocolate-Toffee Crunch

Wendy Anandajeya
Dublin, OH

Make these as a housewarming treat to welcome new neighbors.

1 c. brown sugar, packed
1/2 c. sugar
2 c. all-purpose flour
1/4 t. salt
1/2 c. butter
1 egg, beaten

1 t. baking soda
1 c. buttermilk
1 t. vanilla extract
6 1.4-oz. chocolate-covered
   toffee candy bars, crushed

Combine sugars, flour and salt in a mixing bowl; cut in butter with a pastry cutter until mixture resembles coarse crumbs. Reserve 1/2 cup crumb mixture for topping; set this to the side. Add egg to remaining crumb mixture; set aside. In a medium mixing bowl, blend baking soda and buttermilk together; mix into main crumb mixture. Stir in vanilla; spread in a buttered 13"x9" baking pan. Sprinkle with reserved crumb mixture and crushed candy bars; bake at 350 degrees for 30 minutes. Cool on wire rack; cut into squares to serve. Makes 2 dozen.

When packing cupcakes, brownies or scones to share, tuck between layers of colorful wax tissue paper trimmed with decorative-edged scissors. What a lovely and welcome gift!

Chocolate...Striking It Rich

Triple Chocolate Chippers

Jennifer Dutcher
Gooseberry Patch

Cookies just bursting with flavor!

2 1-oz. sqs. unsweetened
    baking chocolate
1-3/4 c. semi-sweet chocolate
    chips, divided
1/2 c. butter, softened
1 c. sugar

2 eggs
1-1/2 t. vanilla extract
1-1/2 c. all-purpose flour
1/2 c. white chocolate chips
1/4 c. milk chocolate chips
1/4 c. butterscotch chips

Melt chocolate squares and 3/4 cup semi-sweet chocolate chips in a double boiler; stir until smooth and creamy. Pour into a large mixing bowl; blend in butter until thoroughly combined. Add sugar, eggs and vanilla, beating well. Blend in flour; add remaining chips, white chocolate chips, milk chocolate chips and butterscotch chips. Mix at low speed until chips are evenly distributed throughout the dough; drop by heaping tablespoonfuls 2 inches apart on parchment-lined baking sheets. Flatten to 1/2-inch thickness; bake at 375 degrees for 10 to 12 minutes. Remove from baking sheets; cool. Makes about 2-1/2 dozen.

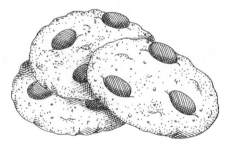

Chocolate shavings look so delicate but are really simple to make. Just pull a vegetable peeler across a bar of chocolate and watch it curl!

Chocolate-Raspberry Truffles

Virginia Garrelts
Salina, KS

This is a "must" at our house!

3 c. chocolate chips, divided
2 T. whipping cream
1 T. butter

2 T. seedless raspberry jam
Optional: powdered sugar

Combine 1-1/2 cups chocolate chips, cream and butter in a double boiler over low heat; stir until melted and smooth. Add raspberry jam; remove from heat and cool. Cover with plastic wrap; freeze for 20 minutes. Shape into balls; freeze until firm. Melt remaining chocolate chips in a double boiler over low heat; using a toothpick, dip balls into melted chocolate. Place on baking sheets; chill until set. Dust with powdered sugar, if desired. Makes about 3 dozen.

Gather best-loved dessert recipes and put them in a family cookbook. Filled with photos, stories and handwritten notes, it will be a treasure to pass down.

Chocolate-Covered Cherry Cookies *Kathy Grashoff*
Fort Wayne, IN

Not the candy, but a deliciously moist cookie instead!

1/2 c. butter	1/2 c. baking cocoa
1 c. sugar	1/4 t. salt
1 egg	1/4 t. baking powder
1-1/2 t. vanilla extract	10-oz. jar maraschino cherries,
1-1/2 c. all-purpose flour	drained, juice reserved

Cream butter, sugar, egg and vanilla together until light and fluffy; add flour, baking cocoa, salt and baking powder. Blend on low speed for one minute; shape into walnut-size balls. Place 2 inches apart on ungreased baking sheets; push one cherry into center of each ball. Bake at 350 degrees 8 to 10 minutes; cool and frost. Makes 2 dozen.

Frosting:

1 c. chocolate chips	1/4 t. salt
1/2 c. sweetened condensed milk	1-1/2 t. reserved cherry juice

Melt chocolate chips with milk in a double boiler; stir until smooth. Remove from heat; add salt and juice. Blend until creamy; use 1/2 teaspoonful per cookie.

Just for fun, throw a nothing-but-chocolate party. Everyone can bring their favorite and you supply lots of icy milk!

Cookie Dough Cheese Ball

Kristie Rigo
Friedens, PA

*A hit with kids of all ages. Try graham crackers, animal crackers
and even chocolate chip cookies dipped in this special treat.*

8-oz. pkg. cream cheese,
   softened
1/2 c. butter, softened
1/4 t. vanilla extract
1/2 c. powdered sugar

3 T. brown sugar, packed
3/4 to 1 c. mini semi-sweet
   chocolate chips
3/4 c. pecans, finely chopped

Blend first 3 ingredients together until creamy; add powdered sugar
and brown sugar, blending well. Fold in chocolate chips; cover and
refrigerate 3 to 4 hours. Shape dough into a ball; wrap in plastic
wrap and refrigerate until firm. Roll in pecans before serving. Makes
about 3 cups.

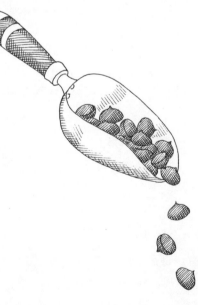

*Pipe melted chocolate into the fork prints on peanut
butter cookies...a winning combination!*

Chocolate...Striking It Rich

Chocolate-Filled Pretzels

Roxanne Heitkamp
Sioux Falls, SD

A simple sweet treat to surprise a classroom of youngsters.

4 doz. pretzel rings
48 milk chocolate drops

1/4 c. candy-coated chocolates

Spread pretzel rings in a single layer on a greased baking sheet; place one chocolate drop in the center of each ring. Bake on lowest oven setting just until chocolate drop is soft, about 2 to 3 minutes; remove from oven. Place one candy-coated chocolate on each chocolate drop; press down slightly until chocolate fills the ring. Refrigerate 5 to 10 minutes until firm. Makes 4 dozen.

Sparklers

Charlotte Smith
Huntingdon, PA

Wrap each in colorful plastic wrap, then tie several together to create a bouquet of yummy treats.

12-oz. pkg. pretzel rods
16-oz. pkg. chocolate chips,
  melted

Garnish: colored jimmies,
  flaked coconut and
  crushed peanuts

Coat top half of pretzel rod in melted chocolate; roll in garnish of choice. Place on wax paper-lined baking sheet; refrigerate until firm.

Short on time but need a dessert fast?
Dip plump strawberries or mandarin orange slices
in melted semi-sweet chocolate. Set on wax paper
and chill until chocolate is firm.

Frozen Mocha Dessert

Janet Miller
Lakewood, CA

This makes enough to serve a crowd!

2 t. instant coffee granules
1 T. hot water
1 c. chocolate sandwich
   cookies, crushed
3/4 c. chopped pecans, divided
1/4 c. butter, melted
2 8-oz. pkgs. cream cheese,
   softened

14-oz. can sweetened
   condensed milk
1/2 c. chocolate syrup
8-oz. container frozen whipped
   topping, thawed

In a small bowl, dissolve coffee in hot water; set aside. Combine cookie crumbs, 1/2 cup pecans and butter in a mixing bowl; press into a 13"x9" baking dish. Blend cream cheese until light and fluffy; add coffee mixture, milk and chocolate syrup. Fold in whipped topping; spread over crust. Sprinkle with remaining pecans; freeze. Makes 24 servings.

A simple treat...dip banana slices into melted chocolate and then roll in mini chocolate chips. Place on a baking sheet and freeze to make a frosty snack.

Brownie-Chocolate Chip Cheesecake

Amy Wellauer
Moravia, NY

Stir in mint chocolate chips for a whole new treat.

20-oz. pkg. brownie mix
3 8-oz. pkgs. cream cheese
14-oz. can sweetened
   condensed milk
3 eggs

2 t. vanilla extract
1/2 c. chocolate chips
Garnish: whipped topping
   and cherries

Prepare brownies according to package directions; pour into a greased 9" springform pan. Bake at 350 degrees for 35 minutes; remove from oven and set aside. Blend cream cheese until light and fluffy; gradually add milk. Mix in eggs and vanilla; fold in chocolate chips and spread over brownie. Reduce oven temperature to 300 degrees; bake for 50 minutes. Cool; refrigerate until set. Remove sides of pan before serving; garnish with whipped topping and cherries. Makes 8 to 10 servings.

I could give up chocolate, but I'm not a quitter.
-Unknown

Simply Delicious Pound Cake

Pamela Voss
Richmond, VA

Pound cake is just pound cake but add chocolate
and it becomes simply delicious!

1 c. butter, softened
2 c. sugar
2 eggs
1 c. sour cream
1/2 t. vanilla extract

2 c. all-purpose flour
1 t. baking powder
1/4 t. salt
6-oz. pkg. chocolate chips

Cream butter and sugar together; beat in eggs, one at a time. Add sour cream and vanilla; blend in flour, baking powder and salt. Fold in chips; spread batter into a greased and floured Bundt® pan. Bake at 350 degrees for one hour; cool for 15 minutes. Remove from pan; cool. Makes 11 to 12 servings.

A house is beautiful not because of its walls,
but because of its cakes.
-Old Russian Proverb

Hot Fudge-Peanut Parfait

Jana Warnell
Kalispell, MT

One bite and your friends will be hooked...everyone will want the recipe!

16-oz. pkg. chocolate sandwich
  cookies, crushed
1/2 c. butter, melted
1/2 gal. vanilla ice cream,
  softened

16 to 18-oz. jar hot fudge sauce
12-oz. can Spanish peanuts
8-oz. container frozen whipped
  topping, thawed

Combine crushed cookies and butter together; press into the bottom of a 13"x9" baking dish. Spread ice cream over crust; freeze until firm. Spoon hot fudge on top; sprinkle with peanuts. Top with whipped topping; freeze until serving, about one hour. Makes 15 servings.

Chocolate cups are yummy filled with fresh fruit. Melt 8 ounces of chocolate and spread inside aluminum foil baking cups. Set cups in muffin tins and refrigerate until firm. To remove, carefully peel off the aluminum foil and refrigerate until ready to fill.

Double-Chocolate Mousse Cake

*Jessica Jones
York, PA*

Don't believe in a flourless cake? Try this!

16-oz. pkg. semi-sweet
   chocolate chips
2 c. butter
1 c. sugar
1 c. half-and-half

1/2 t. salt
1 T. vanilla extract
8 eggs, lightly beaten
Garnish: whipped topping

Place first 6 ingredients in a heavy saucepan; heat over low heat until chocolate chips melt, stirring frequently. Cool to room temperature; fold in eggs. Pour into a greased 9" springform pan; bake at 350 degrees for 45 minutes. Cool to room temperature; spread with topping. Refrigerate until firm; carefully remove pan. Garnish with whipped topping before serving. Makes 10 to 12 servings.

Topping:

1 c. chocolate chips
2 T. butter

3 T. half-and-half
2 T. corn syrup

Melt chocolate chips with butter in a double boiler; remove from heat. Stir in half-and-half and corn syrup; mix until smooth.

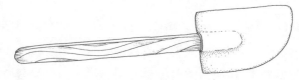

*Does a recipe call for toasted nuts or coconut?
Toast your own by spreading them in a shallow pan
and baking at 350 degrees for 7 to 12 minutes,
stirring frequently until golden.*

County Fair Grand Champion Cake
Cindy Conway
Elizabeth, CO

*You'll never believe the surprise ingredient that makes
this cake a winner...beets!*

2 c. all-purpose flour
2 t. baking soda
1/4 t. salt
3 1-oz. sqs. semi-sweet baking
  chocolate
1 c. oil, divided

2 16-oz. cans beets, drained
1-3/4 c. sugar
3 eggs
1 t. vanilla extract
Garnish: 2 T. powdered sugar

Sift flour, baking soda and salt together; set aside. Melt chocolate
with 1/4 cup oil in a double boiler; set aside. Purée beets; measure
2 cups and set aside. Blend sugar and eggs together in a large bowl;
gradually mix in remaining oil, 2 cups pureéd beets, melted
chocolate and vanilla. Stir in flour mixture; mix well. Grease and
then coat a 10 or 12-cup Bundt® pan with baking cocoa; pour batter
into pan. Bake at 375 degrees for one hour or until toothpick
inserted in center removes clean; cool 15 minutes on a wire rack.
Invert to serving dish; remove pan and dust cake with powdered
sugar. Makes 10 to 12 servings.

*Chocolate whipped cream...just beat 2 tablespoons
each baking cocoa and powdered sugar
into one cup whipping cream!*

Candy Bar Fudge

Susan Brzozowski
Ellicott City, MD

This fudge is more like a candy bar...everyone loves it!

1/2 c. butter, softened
1/3 c. baking cocoa
1/4 c. brown sugar, packed
1/4 c. milk
3-1/2 c. powdered sugar
1 t. vanilla extract

30 caramel candies, unwrapped
1 T. water
2 c. peanuts
1/2 c. semi-sweet chocolate
  chips
1/2 c. milk chocolate chips

Combine first 4 ingredients in a microwave-safe bowl; microwave on high until mixture boils, about 3 minutes. Stir in powdered sugar and vanilla; pour into a buttered 8"x8" baking dish and set aside. In another microwave-safe bowl, heat caramels and water on high for 2 minutes or until melted, stirring after one minute; mix in peanuts. Spread over chocolate mixture; set aside. Melt chocolate chips together; pour evenly over caramel layer. Refrigerate until firm. Makes 2-3/4 pounds.

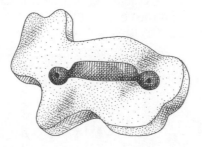

Mini cookie cutters are just the right size to make chocolate cut-outs. Pour melted chocolate onto wax paper-lined cookie sheets and spread to 1/8-inch thickness. Refrigerate until firm and then cut shapes with cookie cutters. Remove from wax paper and chill...a sweet garnish on frosted cakes!

Grandma's Brownies

Robyn Fiedler
Tacoma, WA

A staple at my house when I was growing up...makes enough for 14 grandkids!

1/4 c. butter, melted	1-1/2 c. chocolate syrup
4 eggs	1 c. plus 1 T. all-purpose flour
1 c. sugar	

Combine first 4 ingredients together; blend well. Mix in flour; spread in a greased jelly roll pan. Bake at 350 degrees for 25 minutes; cool. Spread with frosting; cut into squares. Makes 3 dozen.

Frosting:

6 T. butter	1-1/2 c. sugar
6 T. milk	2/3 c. chocolate chips

Bring butter, milk and sugar to a rolling boil in a small saucepan; stir constantly. Remove from heat; stir in chocolate chips until melted and smooth.

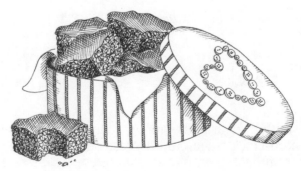

Serve milk in vintage, pint-size milk bottles...such fun at dessert time!

Angel Kisses

JoLisa McCarthy
Bolton, MA

Make before bedtime and then forget about them until morning.

2 egg whites, room temperature
1/2 c. sugar
1 t. almond extract
1/4 t. vanilla extract
1 c. mini chocolate chips
1 c. chopped pecans

Beat egg whites until foamy; blend in sugar until stiff. Add extracts; mix well. Fold in chocolate chips and pecans; drop by teaspoonfuls onto parchment-lined baking sheets. Place in a 350-degree oven; turn oven off and let set 8 to 10 hours or overnight. Do not open door. Makes about 2-1/2 dozen.

Chocolate Brittle

Cynthia Layton
Cape Girardeau, MO

You won't be able to stop munching on this!

2 c. butter
2 c. sugar
1/4 c. plus 2 T. water
12 1.05-oz. milk chocolate
candy bars
3 c. chopped pecans

Combine butter, sugar and water in a Dutch oven; heat until mixture reaches hard-crack stage, 300 degrees on a candy thermometer. Remove from heat; pour into two buttered, 12" pizza pans, spreading to edges. Melt chocolate in a double boiler; spread over brittle and sprinkle with pecans. Let cool; break into pieces. Makes about 4 pounds.

Chocolate Derbies

Laura Lett
Gooseberry Patch

Almost like magic, the oven heat will seal the cookies.

1/2 c. butter
2 T. sugar
1/4 c. brown sugar, packed
1 egg yolk
1-1/3 c. all-purpose flour

1/4 t. salt
1/4 t. baking soda
3 1.55-oz. semi-sweet
     chocolate candy bars,
     chopped

Cream butter thoroughly; gradually add sugars. Blend in egg yolk; set aside. Combine flour, salt and baking soda together in another mixing bowl; add to sugar mixture. Roll dough out on a lightly floured surface to 1/8-inch thickness; cut into 1-1/2 inch circles. Place half of the circles on ungreased baking sheets; sprinkle centers with chopped chocolate. Top each with a remaining circle; bake at 425 degrees for 10 minutes. Remove from baking sheets while still hot; cool on wire racks. Makes 3 dozen.

For even richer tasting hot cocoa,
make it with chocolate milk!

4-Chip Marshmallow Fudge

Jill Moore
Sykesville, MD

A fudge recipe like no other!

3/4 c. butter
14-oz. can sweetened
   condensed milk
3 T. milk
12-oz. pkg. semi-sweet
   chocolate chips
10-oz. pkg. peanut butter chips

12-oz. pkg. milk chocolate
   chips
1 c. butterscotch chips
7-oz. jar marshmallow creme
1-1/2 t. vanilla extract
1/2 t. almond extract

Melt butter in a Dutch oven over low heat; stir in condensed milk and milk. Add chips; stir constantly until melted and smooth. Remove from heat; mix in marshmallow creme and extracts. Pour into a wax paper-lined 15"x10" baking pan; refrigerate until firm. Remove from pan; cut into squares. Makes 3 dozen.

There's nothing better than a good friend,
except a good friend with chocolate.
-Linda Grayson

Chocolate...Striking It Rich

White Confetti Fudge

Angela Nichols
Mt. Airy, NC

I like to keep this on hand...just to snack on.

1-1/2 lbs. white chocolate
14-oz. can sweetened
   condensed milk
1/8 t. salt
1 t. vanilla extract

1/2 c. red candied cherries,
   chopped
1/2 c. green candied cherries,
   chopped

Melt chocolate with milk in a heavy saucepan; stir constantly.
Remove from heat; stir in remaining ingredients. Spread evenly in
a buttered wax paper-lined 8"x8" baking pan; chill until firm. Turn
out onto a cutting board; cut into small squares. Makes 2 dozen.

Delightful No-Cook Fudge

Lisa Smith
Owings, MD

Nothing could be easier!

16-oz. pkg. powdered sugar
1 c. creamy peanut butter
1 t. vanilla extract

3 T. baking cocoa
1 c. butter, melted and cooled

Combine sugar, peanut butter, vanilla and cocoa in a mixing bowl;
add butter. Mix well; spread into a buttered 8"x8" baking pan.
Chill; cut into small squares. Makes 24 servings.

*Spread creamy peanut butter or mint-chocolate
frosting on cooled brownies for a tasty addition.*

Old-Fashioned Chocolate Pudding

Michelle Urdahl
Litchfield, MN

*Made from scratch, this is my mother-in-law's recipe
for a homemade treat the whole family loves.*

3/4 c. sugar
1 T. baking cocoa
2 T. all-purpose flour

2 c. milk
1 t. vanilla extract
Garnish: whipped topping

Combine ingredients in a heavy saucepan over medium heat, stirring constantly; bring to a rolling boil until thickened. Remove from heat; cool. Serve topped with a spoonful of whipped topping. Makes 4 servings.

*Chocolate and raspberry are a heavenly
combination! Try a dollop of raspberry jam
sandwiched between two chocolatey cookies
or warm raspberry jam and spread on fresh-baked
chocolate chip muffins for a no-fuss glaze.*

Chocolate Dumplings

Amy Slikkerveer-Sullivan
North Canton, OH

Tender, sweet dumplings served in chocolate sauce...wonderful!

1-oz. sq. unsweetened baking
   chocolate
1 c. water
1/4 t. salt, divided
2 T. butter, divided
1 c. plus 2 T. sugar, divided
1/2 t. cornstarch
1/2 c. all-purpose flour
1/2 t. baking powder
1 egg
1/4 t. vanilla extract
2 T. milk

Heat chocolate, water, 1/8 teaspoon salt and one tablespoon butter
in a saucepan over medium heat until melted; set aside. Combine
one cup sugar with cornstarch; stir into chocolate. Return to heat for
2 minutes; reduce heat to low, stirring often while mixing
dumplings. In a large mixing bowl, mix flour, baking powder,
remaining salt, sugar and butter together; set aside. Blend egg,
vanilla and milk in another bowl; add to flour mixture. Bring
chocolate mixture to a slight boil; drop in tablespoonfuls of batter.
Cover pan tightly; simmer for 20 minutes. Do not open lid.
Makes 4 servings.

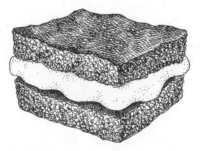

Research tell us that 14 out of any
10 individuals like chocolate.
-Unknown

Triple Chocolatey Brownies

Valerie Beeching
Paw Paw, MI

There's chocolate in the brownie, the filling and the icing!

2 c. sugar
1-1/2 c. all-purpose flour
1/2 c. baking cocoa
1/2 t. salt

1 c. oil
4 eggs
2 t. vanilla extract

Combine sugar, flour, cocoa and salt together; add oil, eggs and vanilla. Blend on medium speed for 3 minutes; pour into a greased 13"x9" baking pan. Bake at 350 degrees for 30 minutes; cool completely. Spread filling over brownie; refrigerate until firm. Drizzle glaze over the top before serving. Makes 3 dozen.

Filling:

1/2 c. butter, softened
1/2 c. brown sugar, packed
1/4 c. sugar
2 T. milk

1 t. vanilla extract
1 c. all-purpose flour
1/2 c. mini chocolate chips

Cream butter and sugars together; add milk and vanilla. Blend in flour until smooth and creamy; fold in chocolate chips.

Glaze:

1 c. semi-sweet chocolate chips   1 T. shortening

Melt together in a double boiler; stir until smooth.

Chocolate...Striking It Rich

Rocky Road Treats

Tina Wright
Atlanta, GA

If you love rocky road ice cream, try these chocolatey squares.

1/2 c. butter, melted
1 c. sugar
1/3 c. baking cocoa
2 eggs
2 t. vanilla extract

1 c. all-purpose flour
1/2 t. baking powder
1/3 c. chopped pecans
Garnish: chopped pecans and
toffee bits

Whisk butter, sugar, cocoa, eggs and vanilla together; add flour and baking powder. Fold in pecans; spread in a greased aluminum foil-lined 9"x9" baking pan. Bake at 350 degrees for 20 minutes; cool. Pour icing over the top; cool. Sprinkle with garnishes; cut into bars. Makes 8 servings.

Icing:

3 T. butter
1/2 c. powdered sugar
1 c. mini marshmallows

2 T. baking cocoa
2 T. milk

Combine ingredients in a heavy saucepan; heat over medium-low heat. Stir until marshmallows melt and mixture is smooth.

One of the secrets of a happy life is continuous small treats.
-Iris Murdoch

Banana-Chip Muffins

Alicia Jordan
Romeo, MI

Really love chocolate? Use chocolate chunks instead of chips!

1/2 c. butter
1/2 c. sugar
1 egg
1 c. bananas, mashed
1 t. baking soda

1 T. hot water
1-1/2 c. all-purpose flour
1/4 t. salt
1/2 t. nutmeg
1/2 c. chocolate chips

Cream butter and sugar together; add egg and bananas, mixing well. In a small bowl, dissolve baking soda in water; add to banana mixture. Stir in remaining ingredients; spoon into paper-lined muffin tins until 2/3 full. Bake at 375 degrees for 18 to 20 minutes. Makes 12.

Create a special message with "balloons." Place frosted cupcakes in a cluster and pipe a single letter on each to spell out a message like "Happy Birthday" or "Good Luck." Tape strands of ribbon to the bottom of each cupcake and tie together with a bow.

White Chocolate Cake

Martha Williams
Louisville, KY

My mother always made this special cake for get-togethers with family & friends. It's moist, with just a little taste of coconut.

1 c. margarine	1 t. baking powder
2 c. sugar	1 c. buttermilk
4 oz. white chocolate, melted	1 c. chopped pecans
4 eggs	1 c. flaked coconut
2-1/2 c. all-purpose flour	1 t. vanilla extract
1/4 t. salt	

Cream margarine and sugar until light and fluffy; add chocolate. Mix in eggs, one at a time, blending well after each addition. In another bowl, combine flour, salt and baking powder together; add to batter alternately with buttermilk. Stir in remaining ingredients; divide and pour into 2 greased and floured 9" round baking pans. Bake at 350 degrees for 45 minutes; cool. Spread with icing. Makes 8 servings.

Icing:

2 c. sugar	1/2 t. salt
1 c. margarine	5-oz. can evaporated milk
1 t. vanilla extract	

Combine ingredients together; mix well. Let stand one hour; stir occasionally. Pour into a saucepan; heat to soft-ball stage, 240 degrees on a candy thermometer. Cool to lukewarm; blend until a desired spreading consistency is achieved.

Mississippi Mud Cake

Violet Hawkins
Perry, MI

So rich and delicious...you just can't resist!

1 c. butter, softened
2 c. sugar
4 eggs
1/3 c. baking cocoa

1-1/2 c. all-purpose flour
1 t. vanilla extract
1 c. chopped pecans
7-oz. jar marshmallow crème

Cream butter, sugar and eggs together; add cocoa, flour and vanilla. Fold in pecans; pour into a greased 13"x9" baking pan. Bake at 350 degrees for 40 to 45 minutes; immediately spread marshmallow creme on hot cake. Set aside 30 minutes; pour frosting on top. Cool until set. Makes 12 to 15 servings.

Frosting:

1/3 c. butter
1/2 c. baking cocoa
2-1/2 c. powdered sugar

1/3 c. milk
1/2 t. vanilla extract

Melt butter with cocoa in a medium saucepan for one minute; remove from heat. Add remaining ingredients; whisk until smooth.

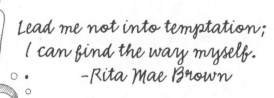

Happy Birthday

Lead me not into temptation;
I can find the way myself.
-Rita Mae Brown

Chocolate... Striking It Rich

Peanut Butter Temptations

Missy Reynolds
Gainesville, FL

You won't be able to keep these bite-size snacks on hand, and since the recipe's easily doubled, you can make a bunch!

1/2 c. butter, softened
1/2 c. crunchy peanut butter
1/2 c. sugar
1/2 c. brown sugar, packed
1 egg
1 t. vanilla extract

3/4 t. baking soda
1/2 t. salt
1-1/4 c. all-purpose flour
48 miniature peanut butter
    cups, unwrapped

Cream butter and peanut butter; blend in sugars, egg and vanilla until light and fluffy. Add baking soda and salt; gradually mix in flour until thoroughly blended. Shape into one-inch balls; place in greased miniature muffin tins. Bake at 350 degrees for 12 minutes; remove from oven. Immediately press a miniature peanut butter cup into the center of each crust; cool completely before removing from pan. Makes about 4 dozen.

Looking for a smooth, velvety chocolate glaze for cookies, cakes or brownies? Melt together one cup chocolate chips with 3 tablespoons corn syrup, 2-1/4 teaspoons water and 1/4 cup shortening. Quick & easy and so good!

Black Forest Cupcakes

Mary Murray
Gooseberry Patch

I like to top these with rich, dark chocolate frosting, but cream cheese or old-fashioned vanilla are just as good.

1 c. all-purpose flour
1/2 t. baking powder
1/2 t. baking soda
1/2 t. salt
6 T. butter, softened
1 c. sugar
2 eggs

2 1-oz. sqs. unsweetened baking chocolate, melted and cooled
1 t. vanilla extract
1/2 c. milk
16-oz. can chocolate frosting
21-oz. can cherry pie filling

Whisk flour, baking powder, baking soda and salt together; set aside. Cream butter on high speed until fluffy; gradually blend in sugar. Continue blending to keep mixture light and fluffy; beat in eggs, one at a time. Add melted chocolate and vanilla; alternately blend in flour mixture and milk until just mixed. Spoon batter into paper-lined muffin tins, filling 2/3 full; bake at 350 degrees for 15 to 20 minutes. Cool 15 minutes on a wire rack before removing; spread with frosting and top with a tablespoonful of cherry pie filling. Makes one dozen.

Melt together 24 ounces semi-sweet chocolate chips, 6 tablespoons corn syrup and one pint whipping cream for a chocolate fondue that's out of this world!

Double-Chocolate Crumble Bars

Brooke Knotts
Cable, OH

A 4-H blue ribbon winner!

3/4 c. sugar
1/2 c. margarine, softened
2 eggs
1 t. vanilla extract
3/4 c. all-purpose flour
1/2 c. chopped pecans
2 T. baking cocoa

1/4 t. baking powder
1/4 t. salt
2 c. mini marshmallows
1 c. chocolate chips
1 c. peanut butter
1-1/2 c. crispy rice cereal

Cream sugar and margarine together in a large mixing bowl; add eggs, one at a time, blending after each addition. Add vanilla; set aside. Combine flour, nuts, cocoa, baking powder and salt together; mix into egg mixture. Spread in a greased 13"x9" baking pan; bake at 350 degrees for 15 minutes. Sprinkle with marshmallows; bake 3 more minutes. Set aside; cool. Combine chocolate chips and peanut butter together in a double boiler; heat until melted and smooth. Stir in cereal; spread over cooled marshmallow layer. Chill until firm; cut into bars. Makes 3 dozen.

A quick & easy get-together idea...invite neighbors over for a dessert buffet. All the goodies can be made ahead of time so they're ready to share when guests arrive.

Best-Ever Turtles

Michele Cutler
Sandy, UT

During the cold winter months when our family makes these,
we're so anxious to eat them that we set the pans of
hot caramel outside to cool!

2 c. pecan halves
1 c. sugar
3/4 c. corn syrup

1 c. whipping cream, divided
4 T. butter
1-1/2 c. chocolate chips, melted

On a baking sheet, arrange pecan halves in sets of three, laying
2 side-by-side and one across the top; set aside. Combine sugar, corn
syrup and 1/2 cup whipping cream in a heavy saucepan; heat over
medium heat, stirring constantly until mixture reaches a full boil.
Slowly add remaining cream and butter; heat until mixture reaches
soft ball stage, or 240 degrees on a candy thermometer. Cool; spoon
a desired amount of caramel mixture on top of each set of pecans.
Let set; dip in melted chocolate. Refrigerate to harden. Makes 2 to
3 dozen.

Top off a chocolatey mug of cocoa with a big dollop
of whipping cream. Set a mini cookie cutter on top
and gently sprinkle cocoa powder inside...carefully
remove the cutter to reveal a special treat.

Chocolate...Striking It Rich

Sweet & Salty Snack Mix

Jennifer Clingan
Fairborn, OH

Sometimes you just have to have both...sweet and salty!

10-oz. pkg. mini pretzels
5 c. doughnut-shaped oat cereal
5 c. bite-size crispy corn cereal
   squares
2 c. salted peanuts

1-lb. pkg. candy-coated
   chocolates
2 12-oz. pkgs. white chocolate
   chips
3 T. oil

Toss together first 5 ingredients; set aside. Melt chips with oil in a double boiler; stir until smooth. Pour over dry mixture; coat completely. Spread mix on wax paper in a single layer; cool. Break apart and store in an airtight container. Makes about 12 cups.

Marshmallow Pops

Judi Gause
Jacksonville Beach, FL

*Keep a variety of holiday sprinkles on hand...a super
quick & easy school or lunch box treat!*

10-oz. pkg. marshmallows
12 popsicle sticks
12-oz. pkg. chocolate chips

2 T. shortening
Garnish: sprinkles, toasted
   coconut, chopped nuts

Thread 2 marshmallows on each popsicle stick; set aside. Melt chocolate chips with shortening in a double boiler; stir well. Dip marshmallows into chocolate; sprinkle with favorite garnish. Lay on wax paper to dry; store in refrigerator. Makes 12 to 18.

Lotsa Hot Cocoa

Lisa Watkins
Gooseberry Patch

Nothing's better...you'll never go back to store-bought again!

1-1/4 c. baking cocoa
1-1/2 c. sugar
3/4 t. salt
1-3/4 c. hot water

4 qts. milk
1 T. vanilla extract
Garnish: whipped topping,
    marshmallows, cinnamon

Combine cocoa, sugar and salt in a 6-quart stockpot; gradually add hot water. Bring to a boil over medium heat for 2 minutes; stir constantly. Pour in milk; heat through but do not boil. Remove from heat; stir in vanilla. Blend mixture until foamy; serve immediately with garnish of choice. Makes about 24 servings.

Iced Chocolate

Melody Taynor
Everett, WA

So refreshing!

3 c. chocolate syrup
2 qts. cold milk
2 t. vanilla extract
2 pts. whipping cream

crushed ice
Garnish: whipped topping and
    maraschino cherries

Blend chocolate syrup, milk and vanilla together in a large mixing bowl; set aside. Whip cream until thick; add to chocolate mixture. Blend until light and frothy; pour into serving glasses half-filled with crushed ice. Top with a dollop of whipped topping and a cherry. Makes 18 servings.

Chocolate...Striking It Rich

Chocolate Popcorn Balls

Annette Ingram
Grand Rapids, MI

Sometimes we add chopped nuts or candy-coated chocolates to the chocolate mixture for even more flavor and crunch.

1-1/4 c. sugar
1/2 c. baking cocoa
3/4 c. corn syrup
2 t. cider vinegar

1/8 t. salt
2 T. butter
1/4 c. evaporated milk
2 qts. popped popcorn

Combine first 5 ingredients together in a heavy saucepan; add butter. Heat over low heat until sugar dissolves; stir constantly. Bring mixture to a boil; slowly pour in evaporated milk so boiling does not stop. Heat until mixture reaches 265 degrees on a candy thermometer; stir occasionally. Remove from heat; pour over popcorn, coating completely. Working quickly and using buttered hands, shape handfuls of popcorn into 4-inch balls; set on wax paper to harden. Wrap individually in wax paper or plastic wrap. Makes about 20.

For a new twist on the traditional gingerbread house, try baked chocolate chip cookie dough instead. For even more whimsy, break apart chocolate bar sections to make shutters and doors!

Orange-Glazed Chocolate Rolls

Geneva Rogers
Gillette, WY

Chocolate flavor with just a hint of citrus
makes these rolls my family's favorite.

3 c. all-purpose flour, divided
2 pkgs. active dry yeast
1 t. salt
1 t. cinnamon
1-1/4 c. water

1/3 c. sugar
1/3 c. butter
1 egg
1/2 c. raisins
1 c. semi-sweet chocolate chips

Combine 1-1/2 cups flour, yeast, salt and cinnamon in a large mixing bowl; set aside. Add water, sugar and butter to a small saucepan; heat, stirring constantly, to 115 to 120 degrees on a candy thermometer or until butter is almost melted. Add to flour mixture; blend until smooth. Mix in egg; stir in remaining flour. Fold in raisins; cover and let rise until double in bulk. Punch down; set aside 10 minutes. Fold in chocolate chips; fill greased muffin tins 2/3 full. Cover; let rise until double in bulk. Bake at 425 degrees for 10 to 15 minutes; let cool completely. Drizzle with glaze before serving. Makes about 1-1/2 dozen.

Glaze:

1/2 c. powdered sugar

3 t. orange juice

Combine until smooth and creamy.

All I really need is love,
but a little chocolate now and
then doesn't hurt!
—Lucy Van Pelt, Peanuts

Ooey gooey treats

Magic Bars

Melanie Heffner
Beaverton, OR

As fast as my Auntie Jo bakes 'em...they disappear!

1/2 c. margarine, melted
1-1/3 c. graham cracker crumbs
14-oz. can sweetened
   condensed milk

1-1/2 c. semi-sweet chocolate
   chips
1-1/2 c. chopped walnuts

Stir margarine and graham cracker crumbs together; press into a
13"x9" glass baking dish. Pour milk over crumb mixture; sprinkle
with chocolate chips and walnuts. Bake at 350 degrees for
25 minutes; cool and cut into squares. Makes 2 dozen.

Queen Annes

Melissa Parcel
Kelso, WA

Your family will feel like royalty when you make these for them!

1-1/4 c. graham crackers,
   crushed
14-oz. can sweetened
   condensed milk

12-oz. pkg. chocolate chips
1 t. vanilla extract
1 c. powdered sugar

Combine first 4 ingredients together; spread in a 9"x9" baking dish.
Bake at 375 degrees for 20 minutes or until golden; cool slightly. Cut
into bars; roll in powdered sugar. Store in an airtight container.
Makes about one dozen.

Ooey-Gooey Treats

Chewy Chocolate-Caramel Bars

Linda Kohrs
Mesa, AZ

These chewy squares will be a hit at any bake sale!

1 c. quick-cooking oats,
    uncooked
1/2 c. brown sugar, packed
1/2 c. sugar
1 c. all-purpose flour
1 t. baking soda

3/4 c. butter, melted
14-oz. pkg. caramels,
    unwrapped
3 T. milk
12-oz. pkg. milk chocolate
    chips

Combine oats, brown sugar, sugar, flour, baking soda and butter; press half of mixture into a greased 9"x9" baking dish. Bake at 350 degrees for 10 minutes. While baking, melt caramels with milk in a double boiler; stir until smooth. Sprinkle chocolate chips over hot crust; pour melted caramel on top. Spread remaining dry mixture over top; bake 15 more minutes. Cool; cut into squares. Makes one dozen.

Say "Welcome!" to new co-workers...leave a basket of candy, cookies or brownies on their desk. If they're new to town, be sure to include directions to all the best places for lunch, the bank and the post office.

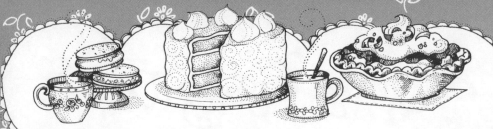

Peaches & Cream Dessert

Beth Ratcliff
West Des Moines, IA

Peaches never tasted so good!

3/4 c. all-purpose flour
3-1/2 oz. pkg. instant vanilla
   pudding mix
1 t. baking powder
1 egg, beaten
1/2 c. milk
3 T. butter, melted

16-oz. can sliced peaches,
   drained, reserving
   1/3 c. juice
8-oz. pkg. cream cheese,
   softened
1/2 c. plus 1 T. sugar, divided
1/2 t. cinnamon

Combine flour, vanilla pudding and baking powder; set aside. Blend egg, milk and butter together; add to dry ingredients. Mix well; spread in a greased 8"x8" baking pan. Chop peaches and sprinkle over batter; set aside. Blend cream cheese, 1/2 cup sugar and reserved peach juice together until smooth; pour over peaches. Mix remaining sugar and cinnamon together; sprinkle on top. Bake at 350 degrees for 45 minutes. Makes 9 servings.

Surprise the kids with a straw they can eat...a piece of licorice!

Ooey-Gooey Treats

Bananas Betty

Debbie Talley
Wichita Falls, TX

Bananas in a creamy hazelnut sauce...yum!

6 T. butter, divided
1/4 c. brown sugar, packed
1/2 c. plus 2 T. all-purpose
    flour, divided
1/4 c. chopped pecans
1/4 t. salt, divided

1/3 c. sugar
1 T. lime juice
2 c. bananas, mashed
1 T. hazelnut flavoring
4 8-inch flour tortillas

Melt 2 tablespoons butter in a small saucepan; add brown sugar, stirring until dissolved. Pour into a mixing bowl; mix in flour, pecans and 1/8 teaspoon salt. Spread onto a parchment paper-lined baking sheet; bake at 350 degrees for 15 to 18 minutes or until golden and crispy. Cool on a wire rack; chop into coarse crumbs. In a skillet, combine remaining butter, sugar, lime juice and remaining salt; heat over low heat until butter melts. Increase heat to medium until mixture begins to brown, about 3 minutes; add bananas and flavoring. Stir to coat bananas; transfer to a 2-quart bowl. Stir in crumb mixture; spoon equally into centers of tortillas. Roll up; place seam-side down in a 13"x9" baking pan. Place in oven on warm setting; heat until tortillas soften. Makes 4 servings.

Baked Bananas...an ooey, gooey treat in minutes! Place unpeeled bananas on a baking sheet and bake at 350 degrees for 20 minutes. Slice skins, mash bananas with a fork and top with vanilla ice cream.

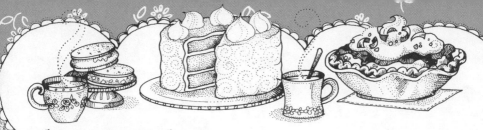

Chewy Caramels

Teresa Velleggia
Monkton, MD

So simple, even the kids can help out.

2 c. corn syrup
1-lb. pkg. brown sugar
14-oz. can sweetened
   condensed milk

1/2 c. butter
Optional: 1 c. chopped nuts

Combine first 4 ingredients in a heavy saucepan; heat over medium heat until soft-ball stage or 240 degrees on a candy thermometer. Remove from heat; stir in nuts, if desired. Pour into a lightly buttered 9"x9" baking pan; cool. Cut and wrap individually in wax paper. Makes about 2-1/2 pounds.

Candy garlands are a colorful way to decorate for a little one's birthday party! Punch a hole in candy wrappers, and then slip a length of ribbon through the holes. Hang several around the edge of the birthday table...they'll soon be gone!

Ooey-Gooey Treats

Chocolate-Butter Cream Squares

Dorothy Armijo
Dallas, TX

Tastes like a combination of brownies and butter cream candy.

1/4 c. butter
1/2 c. sugar
1 egg, beaten
1-oz. sq. unsweetened baking
   chocolate, melted

1/2 c. all-purpose flour
1/4 c. chopped nuts

Cream butter, sugar and egg; add in chocolate, flour and nuts. Spread evenly into an 8"x8" greased and floured baking pan; bake at 350 degrees for 10 minutes. Cool; spread with filling and then icing over the top. Chill until set; cut into small squares. Makes 2 dozen.

Filling:

2 T. margarine, softened
1 c. powdered sugar

1 T. whipping cream
1/2 t. vanilla extract

Blend until smooth and creamy. Refrigerate for 10 minutes before spreading.

Icing:

1-oz. sq. unsweetened baking
   chocolate

1 T. butter or margarine

Melt together in a double boiler; stir until blended.

Raspberry-Coconut Bars

Roberta Lind
APO, England

If you really like raspberries, try raspberry chips instead
of white chocolate...either way, these won't last long.

1-2/3 c. graham cracker crumbs
1/2 c. butter, melted
7-oz. pkg. flaked coconut
14-oz. can sweetened
    condensed milk

1 c. raspberry jam
1/3 c. chopped nuts
1/2 c. chocolate chips, melted
1/2 c. white chocolate chips,
    melted

Mix crumbs and butter together; press into a greased 13"x9" baking pan. Sprinkle with coconut; pour milk over the top. Bake at 350 degrees for 20 minutes; cool. Spread with raspberry jam; refrigerate 3 to 4 hours. Sprinkle with nuts; drizzle with melted chocolates. Chill until serving; cut into small bars. Makes 2 dozen.

Try this fruit smoothie on a hot summer day...just
substitute milk for water in a favorite fruit
juice concentrate. Pour into the blender
with several ice cubes and blend
until frothy. So refreshing!

Golden Lemon Cups

Lori Graham
Pittsfield, PA

*While I was growing up, a special cousin and I would take turns
going to each other's homes on the weekends. One of my favorite
memories is of us playing outside in the snow and then finding
these tasty treats warm from the oven when we returned.*

1 c. sugar
4 T. all-purpose flour
1/8 t. salt
2 T. butter, melted
5 T. lemon juice

zest of 1 lemon
3 eggs, separated and beaten
1-1/2 c. milk

Blend sugar, flour, salt and butter together; add lemon juice and zest,
mixing well. Stir in egg yolks and milk; gently fold in egg whites.
Divide and pour evenly into 8 greased custard cups; place custard
cups in an oven-safe pan of hot water. Bake at 350 degrees for
45 minutes. Makes 8 servings.

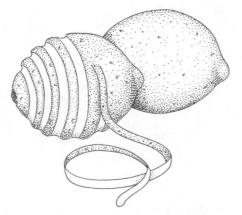

*A plain angel food cake is anything but plain
when the center's filled with fresh fruit and dusted
with powdered sugar...what could
be quicker?*

Cherry Cobbler

Tina Pfeifer
Twentynine Palms, CA

You just can't go wrong with this old-fashioned favorite.

1/2 c. butter, melted
1 c. all-purpose flour
1 c. sugar

1 t. baking powder
1 c. milk
21-oz. can cherry pie filling

Coat bottom of a 13"x9" baking dish with butter; set aside. Combine flour, sugar and baking powder together in a mixing bowl; stir in milk. Pour into baking dish; spread cherry filling over the top, do not stir. Bake at 350 degrees for 50 to 60 minutes. Makes 12 servings.

A full-size graham cracker makes an edible "post-card" party invitation. Just pipe on a message with frosting...delicious!

Ooey-Gooey Treats

Baked Pineapple

Jan Rawlins
Harrison City, PA

This is a favorite of the folks in Western Pennsylvania!

20-oz. can crushed pineapple,
   undrained
1/4 c. water
2 T. cornstarch

2 eggs
1 c. sugar
2 T. margarine or butter
cinnamon to taste

Pour pineapple into a 2-quart baking dish; set aside. Combine water and cornstarch; pour over pineapple. Whisk eggs and sugar together; pour over pineapple mixture. Stir mixture; dot with margarine or butter. Sprinkle with cinnamon; bake at 350 degrees for one hour. Makes 10 to 12 servings.

Banana Bars

Romola Knotts
Woodstock, OH

*Frost with a butter cream frosting and drizzle
with chocolate syrup...delicious!*

1/2 c. butter
1-1/2 c. sugar
2 eggs, beaten
1 c. bananas, mashed
1 t. vanilla extract

2 c. all-purpose flour
1/2 t. salt
1 t. baking soda
3/4 c. buttermilk

Cream butter and sugar together; add eggs. Mix in bananas, vanilla, flour, salt and baking soda; gradually blend in buttermilk. Spread in a greased 15"x10" baking sheet; bake at 350 degrees for 15 to 20 minutes. Cool; cut into squares. Makes 3 dozen.

Pecan Pie Bars

Laura Lett
Gooseberry Patch

Bite-size pecan pies!

2 c. all-purpose flour
1/2 c. sugar
1/8 t. salt
1-1/4 c. butter, sliced and
   divided
1 c. brown sugar, packed

1 c. corn syrup
1/2 c. butter
4 eggs, beaten
2-1/2 c. pecans, ground
1 t. vanilla extract

Combine flour, sugar and salt in a large mixing bowl; cut in 3/4 cup butter with a pastry cutter until very fine crumbs form. Press firmly into a greased 13"x9" baking pan. Bake at 350 degrees for 17 to 20 minutes or until lightly golden; set aside. Add brown sugar, corn syrup and remaining butter to a saucepan; bring to a boil over medium heat, stirring gently. Remove from heat; stir 1/4 of the hot mixture into beaten eggs. Add remaining hot mixture; stir in pecans and vanilla. Pour into crust; bake at 350 degrees for 35 minutes or until set. Cool completely on a wire rack; cut into bars. Makes 16.

One of the sweetest things in life:
a letter from a friend.
-Andy Rooney

Ooey-Gooey Treats

Gooey Nut Pie

Tracy Gresh
Reading, PA

Once I took this dessert to an open house and could only get my pie plate back on one condition...I had to share the recipe!

16-oz. jar dry roasted peanuts, crushed
1/2 c. butter, melted
2/3 c. sugar, divided
1/8 t. salt
1/8 t. baking soda
8-oz. pkg. cream cheese, softened
1-1/2 t. creamy peanut butter

16-oz. container frozen whipped topping, thawed and divided
6-oz. pkg. instant chocolate pudding mix
6-oz. pkg. instant vanilla pudding mix
3 c. cold milk
Garnish: chopped peanuts and chocolate shavings

Combine peanuts, butter, 1/3 cup sugar, salt and baking soda together; spread evenly in a 10"x8" baking dish. Bake at 350 degrees for 20 minutes; cool. Mix cream cheese, peanut butter and one half of the whipped topping together; spread over cooled crust and set aside. Stir remaining ingredients together until smooth; chill until firm. Spread over cream cheese layer; top with remaining whipped topping. Garnish with additional peanuts and chocolate shavings. Chill until set. Makes 18 servings.

Cookie cutters are just right for cutting brownies, fudge or bar cookies into clever shapes.

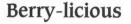

Berry-licious

Virginia Empie
Leeds, UT

If you're looking for a make-ahead dessert, try this...we always think it tastes better the next day.

16-oz. pkg. frozen blackberries
1/2 c. sugar
1/4 c. water
3 T. cornstarch
1 c. chilled butter

1-1/2 c. all-purpose flour
1/2 c. chopped walnuts
1 c. powdered sugar
12 oz. cream cheese, softened
Garnish: whipped topping

Combine blackberries and sugar in a saucepan; boil until sugar dissolves. Whisk water and cornstarch together; add to saucepan. Simmer 3 minutes; cool and set aside. Cut butter into flour with a pastry cutter until mixture resembles fine crumbs; toss in walnuts. Press into an ungreased 13"x9" baking pan; bake at 350 degrees for 15 minutes. Cool; set aside. Blend powdered sugar and cream cheese together until smooth; spread over crust. Pour berry mixture evenly over cream cheese layer; cover with plastic wrap. Refrigerate overnight; cut into squares and serve with a spoonful of whipped topping. Makes 18 servings.

Make your own whipped topping, it's quick & easy! Just beat whipping cream until stiff, adding vanilla extract and sugar to taste...yummy!

Ooey-Gooey Treats

Grapes Supreme

Sandra Kipp
Columbus, OH

A no-fuss dessert that's so refreshing.

1 c. sour cream
8-oz. pkg. cream cheese,
   softened
1 t. vanilla extract

2 T. sugar
2 to 3 lbs. white seedless
   grapes

Combine first 4 ingredients together; mix well. Fold in grapes; stir until coated. Refrigerate for 3 to 4 hours before serving. Makes 8 to 10 servings.

A dessert care package will be a welcome treat for a college student far from home. Send their favorite recipe along with everything needed to make it. Tuck in some already-made goodies too...enough to share!

Brown Sugar Chews

Debbie Long
Sour Lake, TX

Drizzle with maple syrup or sprinkle with
cinnamon & sugar for even more sweetness.

1 c. margarine, melted
2 c. all-purpose flour
1-lb. pkg. brown sugar

2 eggs
1 t. vanilla extract
1-1/2 c. chopped pecans

Mix first 5 ingredients together in order listed; spread in a greased 13"x9" baking dish. Sprinkle with pecans; press down lightly. Bake at 350 degrees for 35 to 40 minutes; cool and cut into squares. Makes 2 dozen.

Create your own sweetheart dessert topper.
Place 2 candy canes on a cookie sheet, arranging
them so they form a heart. Place in a 350-degree
oven for 5 to 10 minutes or just until
they begin to melt together.

Ooey-Gooey Treats

Ooey-Gooey Fondue-y

Cors Burns
Delaware, OH

*A treat from my 7th grade French class. Mom suggests dipping
pineapple chunks, apple wedges, bananas, angel food cake...I
suggest these too, but the best dipper is your finger!*

14-oz. can condensed milk
6-oz. pkg. butterscotch chips
4 1-oz. sqs. unsweetened
   baking chocolate

7-oz. jar marshmallow creme
1/2 c. milk
1 t. vanilla extract

Combine ingredients in a double boiler; heat over low heat until
melted and smooth, stirring often. Pour into a fondue pot; keep
warmed over low heat. Makes 3-1/2 cups.

*Everyone loves dessert pizza! Press ready-made
sugar cookie dough on an ungreased pizza pan and
bake as directed. Let cool, then spread on a mixture
of an 8-ounce package cream cheese,
one cup sugar and one teaspoon vanilla. Top with
fresh fruit and cut into wedges...yummy!*

Cream Puffs

Victoria Bricker
Robesonia, PA

Try this quick & easy recipe to make kids of all ages happy!

1 c. water
1/2 c. butter
1 c. all-purpose flour
4 eggs
6-oz. pkg. instant vanilla
    pudding mix

1 c. milk
2 c. whipping cream
Garnish: powdered sugar

Bring water and butter to a boil in a medium saucepan; stir in flour. Stir vigorously over low heat, about one minute or until mixture forms a ball. Remove from heat; beat in eggs all at once until smooth. Drop by tablespoonfuls onto ungreased baking sheets; bake at 400 degrees for 25 to 30 minutes or until golden. Cool, out of drafts, for 25 minutes or more; cut each in half horizontally. In a mixing bowl, stir pudding and milk together; add whipping cream. Mix well on low speed until thick; refrigerate until firm. Before serving, fill puffs with cream mixture and sprinkle with powdered sugar. Makes 12.

Create a caramel delight to drizzle over ice cream, fruit or cobbler. Heat sugar in a saucepan over medium heat until it begins to turn golden brown...spoon over desserts for a sweet treat.

Ooey-Gooey Treats

Cherry Classic

Kimberly Ward
Middletown, DE

Layer this yummy dessert in a glass bowl...so pretty!

8-oz. pkg. cream cheese,
   softened
3/4 c. powdered sugar
1/2 c. milk
1/3 t. vanilla extract

12-oz. container frozen
   whipped topping, thawed
1 prepared angel food cake,
   cubed
2 21-oz. cans cherry pie filling

Mix cream cheese, sugar and milk together until smooth; add vanilla. Fold in whipped topping; gently mix. Layer half of the angel food cake pieces in bottom of a large glass bowl; spread with half the cream cheese mixture. Top with one can cherry pie filling; repeat layers. Refrigerate 3 to 4 hours before serving. Makes 20 servings.

Melt together 1/2 cup butterscotch chips, 2 tablespoons butter and 2 tablespoons whipping cream, to create a heavenly glaze for any apple dessert.

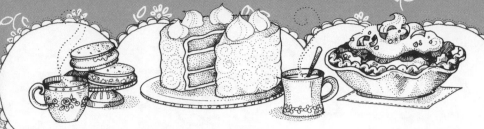

Upside-Down Pecan Loaf

Jackie Balla
Walbridge, OH

Double topping for a truly gooey delight.

3/4 c. butter, melted
1 c. brown sugar, packed
2 c. pecan pieces

4 T. corn syrup
18-1/2 oz. yellow cake mix

Combine first 4 ingredients; divide and spread evenly in 2 greased and floured 9"x5" loaf pans. Set aside. Prepare cake mix as directed on package, using 2 tablespoons less water; pour evenly into loaf pans. Bake at 275 degrees for 55 to 60 minutes; invert pans immediately onto plate or tray with rim. Let stand 2 minutes; remove pans. Slice and serve warm. Makes 16 servings.

*Need a guaranteed bake sale winner? Melt
2 cups peanut butter chips with 2 tablespoons
shortening. Sandwich jam between round buttery
crackers then dip in the melted mixture!*

Ooey-Gooey Treats

Coffee Toffee Bars

Valerie Hugus
Circleville, OH

Just the right size to nibble on.

2-1/2 c. all-purpose flour
1/2 t. baking powder
1/2 t. salt
1 c. butter
1 c. brown sugar, packed

1 t. almond extract
2 T. instant coffee granules
1/2 c. chopped pecans
6-oz. pkg. chocolate chips

Combine all the ingredients together; mix well. Press into a greased 13"x9" baking pan; bake at 350 degrees for 20 to 25 minutes. Cool; frost. Cut into bars. Makes about 2 dozen.

Frosting:

1 T. butter
3/4 c. powdered sugar

1/8 t. almond extract
1 T. water

Blend ingredients until smooth and creamy, adjusting water amount for desired spreading consistency.

Hosting a family reunion? Make bite-size desserts to share...cupcakes, brownies and cookies are easy to snack on while everyone spends time catching up.

Old-Fashioned Caramel Apples

Virginia Watson
Scranton, PA

For a new twist, try dipping the bottom half of caramel-coated apples in melted chocolate and then rolling in nuts.

1 c. sugar
2 c. corn syrup
1/4 t. salt
5-oz. can evaporated milk
1/2 c. warm water

1/8 t. baking soda
1/2 t. vanilla extract
12 large or 20 small tart apples
1 to 2 doz. 4-inch lollipop sticks

Combine sugar, corn syrup and salt in a heavy saucepan; heat over medium heat until mixture boils. In a small mixing bowl, combine milk and warm water; slowly add to sugar mixture. Remove from heat; stir in baking soda and vanilla. Insert lollipop sticks into tops of apples; dip apples into mixture. Place on a lightly buttered baking sheet to cool. Makes 12 to 20.

Crunchy Apple Surprise

Patti Cooper
Gooseberry Patch

A one-serving joy in a bowl!

1 Red Delicious apple, cored
   and sliced
1 t. lemon juice
1/4 c. caramel ice cream
   topping

1 T. peanuts
1 T. honey-roasted peanuts
Garnish: whipped topping

Toss apples with lemon juice in a small serving bowl; lightly mix in remaining ingredients. Top with whipped topping before serving. Makes one serving.

Ooey-Gooey Treats

Candy Apples

Michelle Campen
Peoria, IL

*Stir in a few red cinnamon candies after removing from heat
if you want that added spicy flavor.*

4 c. sugar
1 c. butter
1/4 c. white vinegar
1/4 c. boiling water

1/2 t. red food coloring
10 Granny Smith apples
10 4-inch lollipop sticks
ice water

Combine sugar, butter, vinegar, boiling water and red food coloring
in a large heavy metal saucepan; heat over low heat until sugar
dissolves. Increase heat to medium-high; boil without stirring for
about 10 minutes or until mixture reaches hard-crack stage,
300 degrees on a candy thermometer. Remove from heat; let sit until
bubbles subside. Pierce apples with lollipop sticks; dip into mixture.
Swirl to coat apples; dip into ice water to harden candy coating.
Place on a lightly buttered baking pan until set. Makes about 10.

*I know the look of an apple that is roasting...on
the hearth on a winter's evening, and I know the
comfort that comes from eating it hot, along with
some sugar and a drench of cream.*
-Mark Twain

French Strawberries

Kathy Grashoff
Fort Wayne, IN

*Sweet berries blended with a hint of cinnamon
make this dessert extra-special.*

4 c. strawberries, hulled
   and halved
3 T. frozen orange juice
   concentrate, thawed
1/2 c. plus 2 T. powdered
   sugar, divided

1 c. whipping cream
2 T. sour cream
1/8 t. vanilla extract
1/4 t. cinnamon

Sprinkle strawberries with orange juice concentrate and 1/2 cup
sugar; gently stir. Refrigerate about 1-1/2 hours. In another mixing
bowl, whip cream until soft peaks form; stir in remaining sugar, sour
cream, vanilla and cinnamon. Fold chilled strawberries into whipped
cream mixture. Makes 4 to 6 servings.

*Looking for a sweet & simple snack on the run?
Toss together raisins, banana chips, nuts and
candy-coated chocolates...so tasty!*

Ooey-Gooey Treats

Brown Sugar Fruit Dip

Heather Hood
Bloomville, OH

Stir in crunchy pecans for an added treat.

8-oz. pkg. cream cheese,
   softened
3/4 c. brown sugar, packed
1 c. sour cream
2 t. vanilla extract

2 t. lemon juice
1 c. milk
3-1/2 oz. pkg. instant vanilla
   pudding mix

Blend cream cheese and brown sugar until smooth; add remaining ingredients, mixing well. Cover and chill for at least one hour before serving. Makes about 3-1/2 cups.

Caramel Fruit Dip

Patsy Stembridge
Wylliesburg, VA

We love this with apple and pear slices.

8-oz. pkg. cream cheese,
   softened
1/3 c. brown sugar, packed

1 t. vanilla extract
1/2 t. caramel extract

Blend ingredients together until smooth. Makes about one cup.

Start the day with a flavored cup of coffee for an early sweet treat.

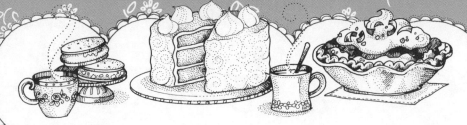

Lemon Bars

Kim Codron
Laguna Niguel, CA

Waves of raves come with this recipe!

1-1/2 c. all-purpose flour	3/4 c. chilled butter, sliced
1/2 c. powdered sugar	Garnish: powdered sugar

Combine flour and powdered sugar; cut in butter with a pastry cutter until crumbly. Press into a lightly greased 13"x9" baking pan; bake at 350 degrees for 15 minutes. Cool. Pour filling over crust; bake at 350 degrees for 20 to 25 minutes or until golden. Cool and cut into bars; sprinkle with additional powdered sugar. Store, covered, in refrigerator. Makes about 2 dozen.

Filling:

4 eggs, beaten	1-1/2 c. sugar
1 t. baking powder	1/2 c. lemon juice
3 T. all-purpose flour	zest of 2 lemons

Blend all ingredients together until smooth and creamy.

Decoupage color copies of wedding photos and sentimental quotes to a paper maché box filled with candy...a heartfelt anniversary gift.

Ooey-Gooey Treats

Peach Cobbler

Kathy Grogg
Lucas, OH

Handed down through many generations in my family,
this recipe was first published in 1863.

4 c. peaches, pitted, peeled
   and sliced
2 T. butter
1-1/2 c. sugar, divided
1/2 c. milk

1/8 t. salt
1 c. all-purpose flour
1 t. vanilla extract
2 t. baking powder
1/2 c. water

Cover bottom of a greased 9"x9" baking pan with peaches; set aside.
Cream butter, 1/2 cup sugar, milk and salt together; add flour, vanilla
and baking powder. Spread batter over peaches; sprinkle with
remaining sugar. Pour water over the top; bake at 350 degrees until
golden, about 45 to 50 minutes. Makes 12 servings.

Best of all are the decorations the grandchildren have
made...fat little stars and rather crooked Santas
shaped out of dough and baked in the oven.
-Gladys Taber

Peanut Butter Fudge

Robin Hutton
Naples, FL

Great as it is or with a little melted chocolate swirled on top.

3/4 c. butter
2/3 c. evaporated milk
3 c. brown sugar, packed

7-oz. jar marshmallow creme
1 c. creamy peanut butter
1 t. vanilla extract

Combine first 3 ingredients together in a heavy saucepan over medium heat; boil for 5 minutes, stirring constantly. Remove from heat; stir in remaining ingredients until melted and smooth. Pour into a lightly buttered 13"x9" pan; cool and cut into squares. Makes 24.

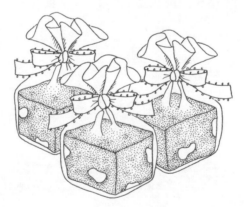

The local 5 & dime always seems to have the best old-fashioned sweets...foil-wrapped coins, candy necklaces and licorice whips!

Ooey-Gooey Treats

Salt Water Taffy

Carol Burns
Gooseberry Patch

The epitome of ooey gooey! Divide and add favorite flavorings and colors to make batches and batches for a rainbow of tastes.

2 c. sugar
1 c. corn syrup
1-1/2 t. salt
1-1/2 c. water

2 T. butter
7 drops green food coloring
1/4 t. peppermint oil

Combine sugar, corn syrup, salt and water in a 2-quart saucepan; heat slowly, stirring constantly until sugar dissolves. Heat to hard-ball stage, 260 degrees on a candy thermometer, without stirring. Remove from heat; mix in remaining ingredients. Pour into a lightly buttered 15"x10" baking sheet or marble slab; cool just until able to handle. Butter hands; gather taffy into a ball and pull. Continue to pull until light in color and hard to pull; divide into fourths. Pull each fourth into a long rope about 1/2-inch thick; cut into one-inch pieces using buttered scissors. Wrap individually in wax paper. Makes 1-1/4 pounds.

Taffy can be any flavor you'd like! Just substitute a favorite flavoring in the recipe...coconut, lemon or butterscotch would all taste terrific.

Blueberry Custard Kuchen

Caroline Capper
Circleville, OH

I live in a "granny house" behind my daughter's family. Every now and then on a Saturday morning, I bake this and invite them over to enjoy a treat. If I wait too long between batches, they remind me that they're getting hungry for it!

1-1/2 c. all-purpose flour,
   divided
1/2 t. salt
1/2 c. cold butter

2 T. whipping cream
1/2 c. sugar
3 c. frozen blueberries

Combine one cup flour and salt together; cut in butter with a pastry cutter until mixture resembles coarse crumbs. Stir in cream; pat into a greased 13"x9" baking pan. Mix remaining flour and sugar together; sprinkle over crust. Arrange blueberries over crust; pour topping over blueberries. Bake at 375 degrees for 40 to 45 minutes or until lightly golden. Serve warm or chilled; store in refrigerator. Makes 10 to 12 servings.

Topping:

1 c. sugar
1 T. all-purpose flour
2 eggs, beaten

1 c. whipping cream
1 t. vanilla extract

Mix sugar and flour together; stir in eggs, cream and vanilla until smooth.

Sugar Cookies
2 c. flour
1 c. sugar
1 c. butter
1 T. Vanilla

Ooey-Gooey Treats

Sweet & Nutty Apples
JoAnn

An old-fashioned favorite...tender apples filled with brown sugar, cinnamon and honey.

1/3 c. chopped walnuts
4 McIntosh apples
1/3 c. brown sugar, packed
2 T. butter, softened

1/2 t. cinnamon
1/3 c. honey
1/2 c. apple juice

Spread walnuts on a baking sheet; bake at 350 degrees until toasted, about 7 minutes. Set aside to cool. Core apples, removing core and seeds to within 1/2 inch from the bottom of the apple; peel top third of apples. In a medium-size mixing bowl, combine brown sugar, butter and cinnamon; toss in toasted walnuts. Spoon equal amounts of filling into each apple; set filled apples in an 8"x8" baking dish. Warm honey in a small saucepan over medium heat; stir until thin. Pour over apples, trying not to pour into cores. Bake at 350 degrees until apples are tender, about 40 minutes; baste two or three times while baking. Cool; serve in bowls with pan juices spooned over the tops. Makes 4 servings.

The friendly cow, all red and white;
I love with all my heart.
She gives me cream with all her might,
to eat with apple tart.
-Robert Louis Stevenson

Pumpkin Squares

*Nikki Olson
Munster, IN*

A favorite during fall, but they're unbeatable any time of year.

4 eggs, beaten
1-2/3 c. sugar
1 c. oil
2 c. all-purpose flour
1-1/2 t. cinnamon

2 t. baking powder
2 t. baking soda
1-lb. can pumpkin
1/2 t. salt
Garnish: colored sprinkles

Mix all ingredients for 2 to 3 minutes or until thoroughly blended; pour into a greased 15"x10" baking pan. Bake at 250 degrees for 50 to 60 minutes; cool. Frost with Cream Cheese Frosting; decorate with sprinkles. Makes 2-1/2 dozen servings.

Cream Cheese Frosting:

1/2 c. margarine, softened
8-oz. pkg. cream cheese,
  softened

2 c. powdered sugar
1-1/2 t. vanilla extract

Combine ingredients until smooth and creamy.

Toss chocolate chips in pancake batter for a gooey breakfast everyone will love...no syrup necessary!

Ooey-Gooey Treats

Peanut Butter Brownies

Naomi Cooper
Delaware, OH

A nice change of pace from chocolate brownies, but you could always top with chocolate frosting for a whole new taste.

1 c. creamy peanut butter
1/2 c. butter
2 c. brown sugar, packed
3 eggs

1 t. vanilla extract
1 c. all-purpose flour
1/2 t. salt

Blend peanut butter and butter together; add brown sugar, eggs and vanilla. Mix until light and fluffy; blend in flour and salt. Spread into a greased 13"x9" baking pan; bake at 350 degrees for 30 to 35 minutes. Cool in pan; frost with peanut butter frosting. Makes 12 servings.

Peanut Butter Frosting:

2 T. creamy peanut butter
2 T. margarine
1 t. vanilla extract

1/8 t. salt
2 T. whipping cream
2 c. powdered sugar

Blend peanut butter and margarine together until fluffy; gradually blend in remaining ingredients until desired spreading consistency is achieved.

Thank a favorite friend with a basketful of mint-chocolate brownies...tie on a silly little note that says, "We were mint to be friends!"

Mocha-Chocolate Steamed Pudding *Sharron Tillman*
Hampton, VA

Don't be intimidated by steamed puddings...they're delicious and surprisingly easy to make. Family & friends will be amazed!

4 1-oz. sqs. unsweetened
   baking chocolate
3/4 c. milk
2 T. instant coffee granules
1/2 c. butter, softened
1 c. sugar

2 eggs, separated
1 t. vanilla extract
1-1/4 c. all-purpose flour
1 t. baking powder
1/4 t. salt

Melt chocolate in a double boiler; stir until smooth. Set aside to cool. In a small saucepan, heat milk and instant coffee until milk is warm and coffee has dissolved completely; set aside to cool. In a large bowl, combine butter and sugar; blend until creamy. Add 2 egg yolks and vanilla; blend well. In another small bowl, combine flour, baking powder and salt; set aside. After milk mixture has cooled completely, blend in alternately with flour mixture to butter mixture. Add the cooled chocolate. In a small bowl, beat egg whites until soft peaks form; stir a small amount of the beaten egg whites into the pudding batter. Carefully fold in remaining egg whites. Pour batter into a steamed pudding mold which has been coated with non-stick vegetable spray. Place on the lid and set the mold on a trivet inside a large stockpot. Pour in boiling water until the water comes up halfway on the pudding mold. Place on medium-low flame and cover the stockpot. Keep the water at a low simmer for 3-1/2 hours; add water as necessary to maintain water level. Remove your mold and let it sit with the lid on for 15 minutes to cool. Remove lid and turn it out onto a plate to cool completely. Pudding should be eaten within one week and should be stored in the refrigerator. Makes 8 to 10 servings.

A sweet centerpiece...place a candle in a pie plate and surround it with peppermint candies.

Ooey-Gooey Treats

Eclair Cake

Cheryl Frost
Woodstock, OH

Luscious cream filling and chocolatey topping...best with a tall, cold glass of milk.

1 c. water
1/2 c. butter
1 c. all-purpose flour
4 eggs, beaten
8-oz. pkg. cream cheese, softened

3 c. milk
2 3-oz. pkgs. instant vanilla pudding mix
Garnish: whipped topping, chocolate syrup

Combine water and butter in a saucepan; heat until boiling. Whisk in flour until smooth; remove from heat. Pour mixture into a mixing bowl; gradually blend in eggs. Spread in a 13"x9" baking pan; bake at 350 degrees for 30 minutes. Remove from oven; press crust down lightly and set aside. Blend cream cheese, milk and pudding together for 2 minutes; spread over crust. Refrigerate until firm. Top with layer of whipped topping and drizzle with chocolate syrup before serving. Makes 12 to 15 servings.

Slice pound cake in 4 layers spreading raspberry jam between each layer. A topping of freshly whipped cream, whole berries and chocolate curls make this oh-so-simple dessert luscious!

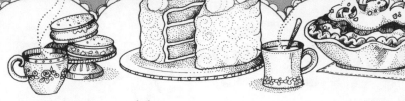

Apricot Crumble

Liz Plotnick-Snay
Gooseberry Patch

Juicy apricots mixed with brown sugar and nutmeg...the kitchen smells wonderful while this is baking.

1 c. biscuit baking mix
1/3 c. milk
1 T. brown sugar, packed
1 T. butter, softened

1/4 t. nutmeg
21-oz. can apricot halves, undrained

Combine all ingredients, except apricots, together until a soft dough is formed. Spread in an ungreased 8"x8" baking pan; pour apricots and syrup over dough. Bake at 400 degrees for 30 minutes. Serves 4 to 6.

Make-ahead desserts, like cobblers or dumplings, are ideal for taking on a family camp-out. Place in a heavy-duty pan and cover with aluminum foil...they'll taste fresh baked as they warm up on the coals after the fire's burned down.

Ice Cream Tacos

Kathy Unruh
Fresno, CA

The kids will love these...they're so fun to eat!

8 frozen round waffles, thawed
1 qt. chocolate ice cream,
   softened

1/2 c. mini marshmallows
1/2 c. hot fudge sauce, warmed
8 maraschino cherries

Warm waffles; do not toast. Gently fold each waffle in half; set in a 13"x9" baking dish open-side up, keeping the rows tight so taco shape is maintained. In a large mixing bowl, combine ice cream and marshmallows; spoon into waffle shells. Drizzle with hot fudge; top each with a cherry. Cover; freeze until firm. Makes 8 servings.

Hot Fudge Ice Cream Topping

Lora Montgomery
Gooseberry Patch

Even when our family diets, I must admit we continue enjoying this recipe on Sunday nights!

1-1/2 c. sugar
1/3 c. baking cocoa
3/4 c. milk

1 t. vanilla extract
1 t. butter

Combine sugar and cocoa in a heavy saucepan; stir in milk until blended. Bring to a boil over medium heat for 5 minutes; remove from heat. Add vanilla and butter; stir to blend. Let mixture cool 2 to 4 minutes; serve over ice cream. Makes about 2-1/2 cups.

We all Scream for Ice Cream

Crunchy Dessert

Lucinda Lewis
Brownstown, IN

*With its butter-pecan flavor and crisp cereal crunch,
everyone will be asking for seconds.*

1/2 c. margarine
1 c. brown sugar, packed
2-1/2 c. bite-size crispy rice
   cereal squares, crushed

3-1/2 c. flaked coconut
1/2 c. chopped pecans
1/2 gal. vanilla ice cream

Melt margarine and brown sugar together in a 10" skillet; add cereal, coconut and pecans. Toast until lightly brown and crisp; stir constantly. Spread half the mixture in an 11"x9" baking pan; set aside. Remove ice cream from carton; slice into 1/2-inch sections. Arrange slices over toasted cereal mixture; seal edges of ice cream together with a spatula. Sprinkle with remaining toasted cereal mixture; cover and freeze until ready to serve. Cut into squares with a knife warmed by running under hot water. Makes 20 servings.

*I doubt the world holds
for anyone a more
soul-stirring surprise
than the first
adventure with ice cream.
-Heywood Brown*

Double Chocolate Ice Cream

Carrie Padgett
Madera, CA

Try using white or dark chocolate-covered sandwich cookies for even more chocolatey goodness.

2 6-oz. pkgs. chocolate
　　pudding mix
3 qts. half-and-half, divided

2 c. chocolate sandwich
　　cookies, coarsely crushed
12-oz. can evaporated milk

Heat pudding and 2 quarts half-and-half until thickened; chill overnight. Pour into a 3-quart ice cream maker; add remaining half-and-half, crushed cookies and enough evaporated milk to reach the fill line. Freeze according to directions of ice cream maker. Makes 3 quarts.

Dirt for dessert? Here's a fun serving idea! Line the inside of a new clay pot with wax paper and then fill with softened ice cream. Cover the ice cream with crushed chocolate cookies and slip a pinwheel in the center. Everyone will love eating their "dirt"!

We all Scream for Ice Cream

Ice Cream Bar Dessert

Karen Cary
Marshalltown, IA

My sister-in-law Kim shared this with me...great for a crowd!

12 ice cream sandwiches	12-oz. jar caramel topping
11-oz. jar hot fudge sauce	8-oz. container frozen whipped
12-oz. pkg. salted peanuts	topping, thawed

Arrange ice cream sandwiches to cover the bottom of a
13"x9" freezer-safe dish; spread with a layer of hot fudge sauce.
Sprinkle peanuts over the top; spread with caramel sauce. Cover
caramel sauce with a layer of whipped topping; freeze. Slice into
squares to serve. Makes 24 servings.

*Toasted walnuts really add flavor and crunch
to any ice cream dessert. Simple to make, just
spread them on a baking sheet and bake at
350 degrees for 10 to 12 minutes.*

Orange Sherbet Dessert

Jennifer Brown
Hillsboro, OR

*Crunchy walnuts and macaroons between two
creamy layers of sherbet...yum!*

1/2 gal. orange sherbet,
   softened and divided
1-1/2 c. macaroon cookies,
   crushed

1 pt. whipping cream, whipped
1 c. chopped walnuts
1 t. vanilla extract
1/2 c. sugar

Spread half the orange sherbet in a 13"x9" glass baking dish; freeze until firm. In a mixing bowl, combine cookie crumbs, whipped cream, nuts, vanilla and sugar; spread over frozen sherbet. Freeze again until firm. Spread remaining orange sherbet over the top; freeze until firm. Makes 24 to 30 servings.

*My advice to you is not to inquire why or whither,
but just enjoy your ice cream while it's on your
plate, that's my philosophy.
-Thornton Wilder*

We all Scream for Ice Cream

Lemonade-Ice Cream Cake

Jennifer Dutcher
Gooseberry Patch

This is my husband's favorite cake...so refreshing and cool on a hot summer day.

18.5-oz. pkg. yellow cake mix
4 c. vanilla ice cream, softened
7 drops yellow food coloring
6-oz. can frozen lemonade
    concentrate, thawed
    and divided

2 c. whipping cream
2-1/2 T. sugar

Prepare cake mix following package instructions for two, 9-inch round cakes; let cool. Combine ice cream, food coloring and 1/2 cup lemonade concentrate; spread evenly in an aluminum foil-lined, 9" round baking pan. Freeze until firm, about 2 to 3 hours. Place one cake round on a serving plate; top with frozen ice cream layer and then remaining cake layer. Freeze. Blend whipping cream with remaining lemonade and sugar until fluffy and peaks form; frost frozen cake. Freeze at least one more hour before serving. Makes 10 servings.

Enjoy s'mores without a campfire! Spread marshmallow creme on whole graham crackers, and then spread with softened rocky road ice cream. Top with another graham cracker, press firmly and freeze until solid.

Pineapple Sherbet

Dianne Gregory
Sheridan, AR

Make your own sherbet...oh-so simple!

1 qt. milk
1-1/2 c. sugar

1/2 c. lemon juice
1 c. crushed pineapple

Scald milk; cool. Add sugar, lemon juice and pineapple; blend well.
Freeze according to ice cream maker's directions. Makes 2 quarts.

Raspberry Pastel Pie

Melinda Spano
Pittsburgh, PA

You can substitute any favorite fruit you'd like.

2 10-oz. pkgs. frozen
    raspberries, thawed
water
6-oz. pkg. raspberry gelatin
    mix

1 qt. vanilla ice cream
2 9-inch graham cracker crusts

Drain raspberries; reserve juice. Add water to juice to equal
2-1/2 cups of liquid; pour into a saucepan. Bring juice and water
to a boil; add gelatin, stirring until dissolved. Gradually spoon in
ice cream; stir until melted. Chill until thick, not set; fold in berries.
Pour equally into two, 9-inch crusts; chill until firm, at least 4 hours.
Makes 12 servings.

We all Scream for Ice Cream

Strawberry Dream

Marylou Loomis
Corry, PA

Cool and frosty!

1 c. strawberries, hulled and
    sliced
2 T. sugar

1 c. plus 2 T. vanilla ice cream,
    softened and divided
2 c. milk

Toss strawberries with sugar; add one cup ice cream and milk. Blend in an electric blender; pour into a tall glass. Spoon remaining ice cream on top before serving. Makes one serving.

Not to like ice cream is to show oneself
uninterested in food.
—Joseph Epstein

Ice Cream Thumbprints

Kris Erdman
Chicago, IL

A delicious twist on a childhood favorite.

2 c. butter, softened
3-1/2 to 4 c. all-purpose flour
1 pt. vanilla ice cream, softened

Garnish: favorite fruit or nut
filling and powdered sugar

Work butter into flour with your hands; gradually mix in ice cream. Combine thoroughly; shape dough into one-inch round balls. Place on ungreased baking sheets; flatten slightly. Lightly press thumb in center of each cookie forming a depression; spoon desired filling into depression. Bake at 350 degrees for 20 to 25 minutes or until golden. Cool; sprinkle with powdered sugar. Makes 3 to 4 dozen.

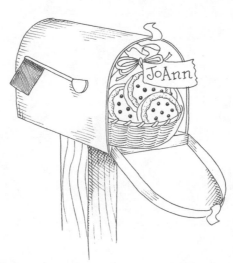

Make birthday cupcakes extra-special. Scoop the centers out of each and use a melon baller to fill the centers with mini scoops of ice cream. Add colorful sprinkles or jimmies for a festive treat!

We all Scream for Ice Cream

Coconut-Almond Dream

Donna Kidd
Bradley, IL

Ice cream tucked between crispy, sweet layers of coconut, almonds and brown sugar...decadent!

2-1/2 c. puffed rice cereal
1 c. brown sugar, packed
1 c. flaked coconut
1-1/2 c. sliced almonds

1/2 c. butter, melted
1/2 gal. vanilla ice cream, softened

Combine first 5 ingredients together; press half of mixture into a 13"x9" baking dish. Spread with ice cream; layer remaining cereal mixture over the ice cream. Freeze until set. Makes 15 servings.

Spoon fruit sherbet in hollowed-out lemons, limes, oranges or melons...they make the prettiest serving "bowls"!

Orange Sherbet Ice Cream

Debbie Crawford
Strafford, MO

Only 2 ingredients...wow!

14-oz. can sweetened
   condensed milk

2 ltrs. orange soda

Combine milk and soda together; mix according to ice cream maker's
instructions. Freeze. Makes about 2 quarts.

Frozen Cherry Yogurt

Megan Brooks
Antioch, TN

Frozen yogurt's a snap to make...give it a try!

4 c. fresh or frozen dark, sweet
   cherries, pitted, thawed and
   divided
8 c. plain yogurt

2 c. whipping cream
1-1/4 c. sugar
2 T. almond extract

Purée half of the cherries; set aside remaining whole cherries.
Combine pureéd cherries with yogurt, whipping cream, sugar and
vanilla; cover and refrigerate 30 minutes. Freeze according to ice
cream maker's instructions; remove to freezer-safe bowl. Stir in
remaining cherries when softened; refreeze until hardened. Makes
4 quarts.

For a new twist, turn a banana cream pie into a
banana split pie! Drizzle slices with hot fudge
topping, nuts and top with a maraschino cherry!

We all Scream for Ice Cream

Rainbow Sherbet Cake

Margie Williams
Gooseberry Patch

Delightfully light and creamy.

1 prepared angel food cake
1 pt. orange sherbet, softened
1 pt. raspberry sherbet,
   softened

1 pt. lime sherbet, softened
12-oz. container frozen
   whipped topping, thawed
Garnish: gumdrops

Slice angel food cake crosswise to make 4 equal layers; place bottom layer on serving plate. Spread orange sherbet evenly over the top; repeat with next two cake layers using raspberry and lime sherbet. Top with final cake layer; frost with whipped topping. Freeze until firm, about one hour. Garnish with gumdrops before serving. Makes 12 to 15 servings.

*I can remember what flavor of ice cream cone
my grandmother and I shared at Disneyworld;
but most of the time, I can't remember what day it is.
I guess it depends on what you think is important.*
—Unknown

Peanut Butter Topping

Merilee Fraser
Muskegon, MI

Drizzle over chocolate ice cream for a peanut butter-chocolate combination that's out of this world!

1 c. brown sugar, packed
1/3 c. milk
1/4 c. corn syrup

1 T. butter, melted
1/4 c. creamy peanut butter

Place brown sugar, milk, corn syrup and butter in a heavy saucepan; heat over medium heat until sugar dissolves. Remove from heat; stir in peanut butter until melted and smooth. Makes about 2 cups.

Chocolate-Peanut Butter Topping

Judy Osborn
Midland, TX

This makes a fabulous milkshake too...just add to taste while the ice cream's in the blender.

8-oz. pkg. chocolate chips
1/4 c. creamy peanut butter

1/4 c. corn syrup
2 T. whipping cream

Melt chocolate chips in a double boiler; mix in peanut butter until smooth and creamy. Remove from heat; stir in corn syrup and cream, mixing well. Serve warm over ice cream. Makes about 1-1/2 cups.

We all Scream for Ice Cream

Classic Vanilla Ice Cream

Teresa Beal
Gooseberry Patch

A basic, old-fashioned recipe that never fails.

1-1/2 c. whipping cream
1-1/2 c. milk
6 egg yolks

2 T. vanilla extract
1/2 c. sugar
1/4 t. salt

Combine cream and milk in a heavy saucepan over medium heat until steam rises; remove from heat and set aside. In a mixing bowl, blend egg yolks, vanilla, sugar and salt together until smooth; gradually pour into warm cream mixture. Heat over medium-low setting; stir constantly until thick, about 6 minutes. Do not boil. Pour through a sieve into a bowl; refrigerate one hour. Freeze according to ice cream maker's instructions. Makes 4 to 6 servings.

A sweet treat for a lazy summer afternoon...ice cream floats! Frosty glasses filled with scoops of vanilla ice cream topped with root beer, red or orange soda will be a hit.

Ice Cream Roll

Jeanne Heykoop
Fostoria, OH

Made like a traditional pumpkin roll, but it's
a chocolatey ice cream-filled cake.

4 eggs, separated
3/4 c. sugar
1 t. vanilla extract
3/4 c. cake flour

1/4 c. baking cocoa
3/4 t. baking powder
1/4 t. salt
3 c. ice cream, softened

Beat egg yolks until light and fluffy, about 3 minutes; gradually add sugar and vanilla. Blend well; set aside. In another mixing bowl, mix flour, cocoa and baking powder together; slowly add to egg mixture. Beat egg whites until soft peaks form; fold a small amount into egg mixture. Add remaining egg whites; spread batter evenly in a greased and floured wax paper-lined 15"x10" baking sheet. Bake at 350 degrees for 15 minutes; turn out onto a linen towel dusted with powdered sugar. Peel off wax paper; roll up cake and towel. Set aside to cool for 30 minutes; unroll cake. Spread with ice cream; roll up again, without the towel. Cover with plastic wrap; freeze until firm. Slice and drizzle with chocolate syrup before serving. Makes 18 servings.

Cake doughnuts make a yummy ice cream sandwich. Cut a doughnut in half and add a scoop of softened ice cream between the two halves. Place on a baking sheet and freeze for one hour...tasty!

We all Scream for Ice Cream

Chocolatey Ice Cream Cookies

Rita Morgan
Pueblo, CO

Round, chocolatey, ice cream-filled treats!

1 c. butter, softened
1-1/4 c. powdered sugar
4 egg yolks
2 t. vanilla extract
2 1-oz. sqs. unsweetened
    baking chocolate, melted

3 c. all-purpose flour
1 qt. ice cream, softened
Optional: powdered sugar

Cream butter and sugar together; add egg yolks, vanilla and chocolate. Blend well; mix in flour. Divide dough into quarters; shape each quarter into a log, 1-1/2 inches in diameter. Wrap in plastic wrap; refrigerate until firm, about 30 minutes. Slice rolls into 1/8-inch thick slices; place 2 inches apart on parchment-lined baking sheets. Bake at 350 degrees for 8 to 10 minutes; remove to wire racks. Cool completely; dust with powdered sugar, if desired. Spread several tablespoons ice cream on flat or bottom sides of half the cookies; top with remaining cookies, bottom-side down to form sandwiches. Serve immediately. Makes about 4 dozen.

Snowballs

Tina Stidam
Ashley, OH

With this recipe, it's easy to enjoy a snowball on a hot summer day!

1 qt. vanilla ice cream
2-1/2 c. flaked coconut

Optional: chocolate syrup

Scoop large rounded scoops of ice cream; roll in coconut. Lightly pat coconut into ice cream; place on a wax paper-lined baking sheet. Cover with plastic wrap; freeze at least 2 hours. Drizzle with chocolate syrup before serving, if desired. Makes 4 to 6 servings.

Homemade Ice Cream in a Bag

Stefanie Schroeder
Bay City, TX

Need a classroom treat? This works. Remember the spoons because this can be eaten right out of the bag!

1 c. milk
1 T. sugar
1 t. vanilla extract
ice
1/2 c. rock salt

1-pt. plastic zipping bag
1/2-gal. plastic zipping bag
Garnish: flavored syrup and
    sprinkles

Pour milk, sugar and vanilla into a pint-size bag; seal. Fill larger bag halfway full with ice; pour rock salt on top. Place small bag inside large bag; seal large bag. Shake bags for 10 to 15 minutes, or until ice cream forms; remove small bag and rinse under cold water. Garnish with flavored syrup or sprinkles. Makes one serving.

We all Scream for Ice Cream

Apple Dazzle

Susan Moore
Haymarket, VA

*I called this recipe Apple Dazzle because you'll truly dazzle your
family & friends with this apple-filled ice cream topping.*

1/2 c. butter, melted
3/4 c. brown sugar, packed
1/2 t. cinnamon
1/4 t. nutmeg
1/8 t. salt

4 c. bread, crusts trimmed
4 c. Granny Smith apples,
   cored, peeled and sliced
1 qt. vanilla ice cream

Combine first 5 ingredients; set aside. Cube bread; gently mix into
spice mixture. Layer spice mixture and apple slices several times in a
slow cooker; heat on high setting for 1-1/2 to 2-1/2 hours. Spoon
one or two scoops of ice cream in each of 6 bowls; top with apple
mixture. Serve warm. Makes 4 to 6 servings.

*Turn a chocolate doughnut into a
double-chocolatey treat! Slice a doughnut in
half, fill with softened chocolate ice cream
and then replace the second slice...easy!*

Banana Split Ice Cream

Janet Pastrick
Gooseberry Patch

Once you try this, you'll love it!

5 c. milk, divided
4 egg yolks
2 14-oz. cans sweetened
   condensed milk
2 c. bananas, mashed
2 T. lime juice

2-1/2 T. vanilla extract
3/4 c. chocolate syrup
1/2 c. chopped pecans, toasted
1/3 c. maraschino cherries,
   halved

Combine 2-1/2 cups milk and egg yolks in a heavy saucepan; stir well with a whisk. Cook over medium heat for 10 minutes or until mixture thickens and coats a spoon; stir constantly. Do not let boil; remove from heat. Pour egg yolk mixture, remaining milk and condensed milk into a large mixing bowl; stir well. Cover; chill completely. Add banana, lime juice and vanilla; blend well. Pour into an ice cream maker; freeze according to manufacturer's directions. Spoon ice cream into a 13"x9" freezer-safe container; allow to soften. Gently fold in syrup, pecans and cherries; cover and freeze for 2 hours or until firm. Makes 24 servings.

Make banana splits easier for little fingers to pick up. Instead of slicing the bananas lengthwise, slice them into circles, and then top with ice cream, hot fudge and whipped cream.

We all Scream for Ice Cream

Easy Ice Cream Treats

Barbara Spilsbury
Hacienda Heights, CA

Even the kids can make this!

18-1/2 oz. pkg. chocolate cake
   mix

4 c. vanilla ice cream, softened

Mix cake mix according to package directions, omitting eggs. Drop by heaping tablespoonfuls onto greased baking sheets; bake at 350 degrees for 15 minutes. Cool completely. Spread ice cream on the flat bottom side of half the cookies; top with remaining cookies, bottom-side down. Gently press to form a sandwich; wrap individually and freeze. Makes 6 servings.

Top a warm, flaky waffle with vanilla ice cream, chocolate syrup and a dollop of whipped cream to create a tasty waffle sundae!

Butter-Pecan Sauce

Julie Madsen
Webster, TX

Spoon into a vintage jar and tuck in a basket along with some waffle or sugar cones…this makes a welcome gift.

1/2 c. sugar
1/8 t. salt
1/4 c. evaporated milk

1 T. butter
1/2 t. vanilla extract
1/2 c. chopped pecans

Heat sugar in a heavy saucepan over low heat; stir until dissolved and caramelized or golden. Whisk in salt and milk; stir until smooth. Remove from heat; add butter, vanilla and pecans. Serve warm over ice cream. Makes about one cup.

Vanilla ice cream can become so many different flavors…add crushed peppermint candies, chocolate chips, maple syrup or crushed peanut brittle to softened ice cream. Stir to blend and re-freeze, it's that easy to create brand new favorites!

We all Scream for Ice Cream

Butter-Pecan Ice Cream

Marla Caldwell
Forest, IN

What is it about this classic that makes it so popular? It seems no one can resist the combination of brown sugar and pecans.

1 c. chopped pecans
1/2 c. sugar
2 T. butter
4 c. half-and-half

2 c. brown sugar, packed
4 t. vanilla extract
4 c. whipping cream

Combine pecans, sugar and butter in a heavy 8" skillet; stir constantly over medium heat until sugar dissolves and caramelizes, about 6 to 8 minutes. Remove from heat; spread nuts on a buttered baking sheet and separate into clusters. Set aside; cool completely. Combine half-and-half, brown sugar and vanilla in a large mixing bowl; stir until sugar dissolves. Fold in pecan mixture and whipping cream; freeze in a 4- or 5-quart ice cream maker according to its instructions. Once formed, freeze another 4 hours before serving. Makes about 3-1/2 quarts.

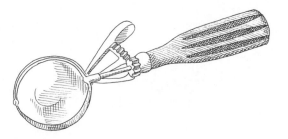

Delight the kids with ice cream sandwiches! Spread a generous amount of softened ice cream over a cookie, top with a second cookie and freeze one hour.

Chilled Vanilla Pudding Cake

Lisa Peterson
Sabina, OH

*Find your family's favorite...combine different flavors of
pudding and ice cream to create a whole new dessert!*

2 3-1/2 oz. pkgs. instant
   vanilla pudding mix
1-1/2 c. milk
1 qt. vanilla ice cream, softened
3 c. round buttery crackers,
   crushed

3 T. sugar
1/2 c. margarine, melted
8-oz. container frozen whipped
   topping, thawed

Combine pudding and milk together until thick; stir in ice cream and
set aside. In another mixing bowl, mix cracker crumbs, sugar and
margarine together; layer half of crumb mixture in bottom of a
13"x9" pan. Layer ice cream mixture, whipped topping and
remaining crumb mixture on top; refrigerate one to 2 hours, or until
firm. Makes 15 servings.

*Make ice cream cones extra-special. Melt chocolate
in a double boiler and dip the top halves of sugar or
waffle cones in the chocolate, swirling to coat well.
Carefully remove cones and immediately roll in
chopped nuts or sprinkles; set on wax paper until
chocolate hardens...what a treat!*

We all Scream for Ice Cream

Frozen Pumpkin Pie

Kim Wacht
Twin Falls, ID

A chilly twist on a traditional favorite.

3 c. vanilla ice cream, softened
1 c. canned pumpkin
1/2 c. brown sugar, packed
1/4 t. salt

1/4 t. cinnamon
1/4 t. ground ginger
1/4 t. nutmeg
9-inch graham cracker pie crust

Combine first 7 ingredients; mix well. Pour into crust; freeze until firm, about 4 hours. Serves 8.

Pumpkin Ice Cream

Sandi Grock
Huntsville, TX

Just for fun, serve this in hollowed-out mini pumpkins!

1 c. canned pumpkin
1/4 t. pumpkin pie spice

1 qt. vanilla ice cream, softened
Garnish: gingersnaps

Combine pumpkin and pumpkin pie spice; stir in ice cream until well blended. Freeze until hardened; serve with gingersnaps. Makes 4 to 6 servings.

Velvety Lime Squares

Kathy Unruh
Fresno, CA

A variety of ingredients come together to make this spectacular dessert. You'll agree, it's a hit!

3-oz. can flaked coconut, divided
2 c. vanilla wafer crumbs
2 T. butter, melted
2 T. sugar
2 3-oz. pkgs. lime gelatin mix
2 c. boiling water

6-oz. can frozen limeade concentrate
3 pts. vanilla ice cream, softened
1/8 t. salt
3 drops green food coloring
Optional: slivered pecans

Spread 1/2 cup coconut on a baking sheet; toast at 375 degrees until lightly golden, about 5 minutes. Set aside. Combine remaining coconut, vanilla wafer crumbs, butter and sugar; press into a 11"x7" baking pan. Bake at 375 degrees for 6 to 7 minutes; cool. Dissolve gelatin in boiling water; add limeade, ice cream, salt and food coloring, stirring until smooth. Pour into crust; sprinkle with toasted coconut and pecans, if desired. Cover tightly; freeze until firm. Let stand at room temperature 20 minutes; cut into squares to serve. Makes 15 servings.

Throw a sundae party to cool off on a hot summer day! Make lots of homemade ice cream and invite friends to bring their favorite toppings to share.

We all Scream for Ice Cream

Homemade Maraschino Cherries
Liz Plotnick-Snay
Gooseberry Patch

*Really simple to make...they're juicier and
better tasting than store-bought.*

1 T. alum
4 T. kosher or pickling salt
cold water
10 c. Royal Anne cherries,
    pitted

7 c. sugar
2 T. red food coloring
1 t. almond extract
1 t. vanilla extract

Dissolve alum and salt in 2 quarts cold water; add cherries. Set aside
for 6 hours; drain and rinse with cold water. In a large saucepan, add
sugar to 2 cups water; boil until sugar dissolves. Stir in cherries;
boil for 2 minutes. Remove from heat; add food coloring and
extracts. Let stand in a cool place for 24 hours; stir occasionally.
Bring mixture back to a boil for 2 minutes; pour into sterilized
half-pint jars, add lids and tighten down rings. Process in a water
bath for 5 minutes. Store in a cool place. Makes about
8, half-pint jars.

When making homemade jam, save some of the
fruit mixture and refrigerate...it makes
terrific ice cream topping.

Frozen Peach Yogurt

Gretchen Miller
Kearney, MO

A light, refreshing dessert that's very tasty.

1 envelope unflavored
   gelatin mix
1 c. milk
1/2 c. sugar
1 t. salt

2-1/2 c. vanilla yogurt
2 t. vanilla extract
3 c. peaches, pitted, peeled,
   and puréed

Sprinkle gelatin over milk in a saucepan; let stand one minute. Heat over low heat until dissolved, stirring constantly; remove from heat. Add sugar and salt; stir to dissolve. Mix in yogurt, vanilla and peaches; cover and chill. Pour into ice cream maker; mix according to its instructions. Makes 4 to 6 servings.

Celebrate Independence Day with a patriotic milk shake! Blend one quart of strawberry ice cream with one cup of milk and 1/2 cup strawberry preserves. Spoon into tall glasses, add whipped cream and top with fresh blueberries.

Frosty Peaches & Cream

Vickie

Frozen yogurt can easily be used in place of ice cream...try peach, it's doubly delicious!

1/2 gal. vanilla ice cream, softened
1 c. peaches, pitted, peeled and puréed
2 T. honey
3 T. sugar

1 t. lemon juice
1 t. vanilla extract
3 T. water
7-oz. jar marshmallow creme
1 c. whipping cream
Garnish: sliced peaches

Spread ice cream evenly in bottom of 13"x9" freezer-proof dish; cover and freeze until firm. Combine peaches, honey, sugar, lemon juice and vanilla together; set aside for 20 minutes. Gradually whisk water into marshmallow creme in a large mixing bowl; add peach mixture. Chill until thickened, about 30 minutes. Lightly whip cream; fold into peach mixture. Spread over ice cream; cover and freeze until firm, about 3 hours. Serve topped with a peach slice. Makes 12 servings.

An incredible treat...fill flat-bottomed ice cream cones half-full of brownie batter, place on a baking sheet and bake at 350 degrees for 20 minutes. When cooled, top with scoops of ice cream!

Index

Index

Index

We've cooked up a whole collection of Gooseberry Patch® books!

Have a taste for more? Call us toll-free at

1-800-854-6673

We'll send you our latest catalog filled with snowmen, Santas, ornaments, candles, cookie cutters, gourmet goodies, calendars, giftwrap, pottery, collectibles and MORE...including our best-selling cookbooks!

Phone us:
1·800·854·6673

Fax us:
1·740·363·7225

Visit our website:
gooseberrypatch.com

Send us your favorite recipe!

Include the memory that makes it special for you too! If we select your recipe for a brand new **Gooseberry Patch** cookbook, your name will appear right along with it...and you'll receive a FREE copy of the book! Mail to:

Vickie & Jo Ann
Gooseberry Patch, Dept. Book
600 London Road
Delaware, Ohio 43015

*Please include the number of servings and all other necessary information!

cupcakes cookies Goodies sweet treats

candies Pies ice cream Brownies Butter cream FROSTING VANILLA

HOMEMADE à la MODE caraMeL second-HeLPiNGS PUDDiNG CRAViNG!

CHOCOLATE Gooey-GooD MeRiNGUe cupcakes